CLASSIFIED

CLASSIFIED

HIDDEN TRUTHS IN THE ISRO SPY STORY

J. RAJASEKHARAN NAIR

Srishti
PUBLISHERS & DISTRIBUTORS

Srishti Publishers & Distributors
A unit of AJR Publishing LLP
212A, Peacock Lane
Shahpur Jat, New Delhi – 110 049
editorial@srishtipublishers.com

First published by
Srishti Publishers & Distributors in 2022

10 9 8 7 6 5 4 3 2 1

This is a work of non-fiction, based on the author's experiences. The views and opinions expressed in this book are the author's own and the facts are as reported by him. They have been verified at press time to the extent possible, and the publishers shall not be held liable for the same.

Printed and bound in India

To my parents,

To my sister,

To Aamy, my best friend,

To my soulmate.

"Democracy needs the power of truth to survive... One cannot solely rely on the State to determine the truth as citizens also play an important role in it."

– Justice D.Y. Chandrachud
(28 August 2021)

Contents

Acknowledgement

Towards the fag end of May, I got a WhatsApp message from Ms Dipti Patel, my literary agent, inquiring about the possibility of a sequel to my book *Spies from Space: The ISRO Frame-up* (1998). One month later, I sent her the manuscript of *Classified*. My thanks to Ms Dipti Patel.

My thanks to Mr Arup Bose, who brought out the book in record time, considering the topicality of the subject.

My thanks to Ms Stuti for editing and polishing my manuscript and for suggesting the present title.

I thank my friend R. Gopalakrishnan for converting hundreds of pages of scanned documents to Word.

During this time, I contracted COVID 19 and my condition was critical. The virus taught me how a microscopic entity could undo our social, moral and spiritual values. My thanks to the virus for teaching me a great lesson no scripture or philosophical treatise taught me.

Prologue

Twenty-seven years after it hit the headlines, the Indian Space Research Organisation (ISRO) espionage case is still alive and kicking. This time, with Central Bureau of Investigation (CBI) registering the First Information Report (FIR) before the Chief Judicial Magistrate (CJM), Thiruvananthapuram, against seven Kerala Police officers and eleven officers from IB, all retired, for conspiring to effectuate the illegal arrest and subsequent torture of S. Nambi Narayanan, one of the six discharged 'accused' in the spy case (1994).

The new development has pushed the public into a mire of contrived truths. That's partly because of the asinine and disgusting move to project the espionage case as the sad story of S. Nambi Narayanan, effacing even the names of the other five victims – two of whom are no more – from public memory. It is also because of the stealthy manner in which the state agencies had reacted to the case then and now, and partly because of the hidden fractures in our system.

The latest FIR paints the old heroes as 'villains', and the media hail the old villains as 'heroes'. It's like scripting a comedy of errors, while the state agencies surreptitiously bury the wreckage of a failed reverse espionage – jointly planned by Glavkosmos, the Russian space organization, and the ISRO top brass and its technocrats, including S. Nambi Narayanan and D. Sasikumaran, to illegally transfer the cryogenic rocket technology from Glavkosmos to ISRO. It was done with the tacit support of the Russian government, hoodwinking the Central

Intelligence Agency (CIA), after the ISRO-Glavkosmos agreement of 1991 to legally transfer the cryogenic rocket technology was scrapped by the Russian government in 1993, invoking *force majeure*, under severe pressure from the US administration.

Besides, furtive efforts are on to efface the remnants of the master plan of a clandestine operation, jointly conceived by Glavkosmos and ISRO. They had planned to use KELTEC (now, BrahMos Aerospace) at Thiruvananthapuram as a conduit to outwit the amended provisions of Missile Technology Control Regime (MTCR) and facilitate the transfer of cryogenic rocket technology to ISRO in an illegal manner.

Meanwhile, the FIR has set the stage ready for yet another high-voltage drama with the courts in Kerala witnessing allegations and counter-allegations between the old villains and the new villains. And sadly, all that has nothing to do with the meat of the spy case.

If the ISRO spy case was false and baseless, as the CBI concluded after eighteen months of investigation, don't we have the right to know who planted it?

If ISRO didn't have cryogenic rocket technology in 1994 – when it was alleged to have been sold to Pakistan by two technocrats in ISRO with the help of two semi-literate Maldivian women – why didn't the chairman of ISRO, the Space Commission or the Department of Space dismiss it as rubbish and nipped the absurd spy story in the bud on the first day itself? Why did they keep their mouths shut even when the nation's pride and ISRO's credibility were trampled upon and kicked on the street?

Interestingly, ISRO tweeted on 29 July 2021 that its chairman, Dr K. Sivan has formally launched its theme-based merchandise, including T-shirts, and claimed "customized ISRO-theme-based products can play a game-changing role in creating awareness and kindling the interest of the students, children and public in the domain of space science and technology, propagating the achievements and laurels that ISRO brings to the nation."

I wonder what prevented the then Chairman Dr K. Kasturirangan from holding a press conference, in the first week of November 1994 itself, and telling the truth to the nation – that ISRO didn't have the cryogenic rocket technology when it was alleged to have been leaked to Pakistan!

Had he done that – something you expect any officer of substance would do – he could have arrested the spread of lies churned out by the media and saved ISRO from the damage the espionage case caused it.

But then, why didn't he do it? Did some agency bully him not to tell the truth? Did he really fear that he would be opening a can of worms if he dared to bust the absurd espionage story?

Why didn't the editors, who sent reporters to the Maldives to collect information on the Maldivian women, send at least a cub reporter to VSSC, just eleven kilometers from the heart of Thiruvananthapuram, to enquire whether ISRO had cryogenic rocket technology in 1994?

As we delve into the spy case, more intriguing questions surface.

What was the legal authority of Kerala Police to register a case under the Indian Official Secrets Act (IOS), 1923, on a crime of spying in ISRO, a Central government organization?

How could the CBI investigate the espionage case in the absence of a formal complaint from ISRO or the Central government reaching the competent Magistrate?

How could Intelligence Bureau (IB), a ghost organization with no legal legitimacy to justify even its existence in the post-Independence India, interrogate and torture the accused persons while under police custody?

How could two learned judges of the Kerala High Court put on record that "IB which has its own investigation machinery" in a crucial judgment in 1995, in a case connected to the ISRO spy case? How could the senior high court judges be that ignorant about the law of the land?

Why did the Supreme Court of India, through its judgment of 14 September 2018, make the espionage case appear to be the illegal arrest and torture of S. Nambi Narayanan, obliterating the transnational dimensions of a highly complex and equally complicated espionage case that had damning ramifications on the domestic front, exposing the truth of our premier institutions?

If it is proved beyond doubt that the custody of all the six accused was illegal – which is indeed what happened in the ISRO espionage case – doesn't the state, of which the judiciary is an integral part, own a responsibility to order compensation for all wrongly accused?

Addressing the question, Justice Madan B. Lokur said, "How can people deal with this situation? The only answer is accountability, which has to be in two forms – One is financial accountability where a sufficient amount of compensation must be given. If S. Nambi Narayanan can be given fifty lakh rupees, surely a good amount of compensation can be given to all those people who have been wrongly arrested and detained. Once the courts start telling the police or the prosecution that you are bound to pay, I think they will probably come to their senses and not make unnecessary arrests. This is one aspect."[1]

S. Nambi Narayanan was in custody for 50 days. But it cannot be ignored that D. Sasikumaran, a former ISRO Engineer of equal stature, was under custody for 60 days; K. Chandrasekhar, agent of Glavkosmos, was under custody for 58 days; Sudhir Kumar Sharma, a labour contractor who didn't even know the full form of ISRO when

1. *Live Law.in*, 22 August 2021

he was arrested, was under custody for 49 days; Fauziya Hassan, a Maldivian woman was under custody for 1000 days; and Marian Rasheeda, another Maldivian woman, was under custody for 1145 days. All the five were brutally tortured under illegal custody.

Then, why didn't the Supreme Court think it was prudent to compensate all and not just S. Nambi Narayanan, one of the discharged 'accused', whose suit for damages (O.S. No.370/2003) to the tune of one crore rupees was pending before the sub-court in Thiruvananthapuram?[2]

Incidentally, the National Human Rights Commission (NHRC) also did a similar act of justice and magnanimity in the ISRO espionage case when it directed the Kerala government on 14 March 2001 to pay ten lakh rupees as 'immediate interim relief' to S. Nambi Narayanan as 'compensation for gross violation of his human rights by public servants'. It is pertinent to note that the same NHRC had rejected two earlier petitions filed by Mariam Rasheeda and Fauziya Hassan, co-accused in the same espionage case.

Don't these acts of justice and magnanimity exemplify the inherent fault in our system? Quite often, it pulls the wool over a thousand system failures by correcting one glaring error that is bound to get much public attention and hail it as the inherent nature of the system.

While these questions remain unanswered, many more are emerging afresh from the residue, like killer germs that leave the corpse in search of the living ones.

Do we need social distancing from these critical questions? Why should we desensitize our prudence using patriotic sanitizers?

---

2. S. Nambi Narayanan withdrew the suit in 2019, 15 months after the Supreme Court had ordered Rs. 50 lakh compensation for him, and accepted Rs. 1.3 crore from Kerala government for an out-of-court settlement

Why should the media mask these loaded questions and focus on personality-hype interviews instead?

The state agencies that should have shown us the truth hold a black paper in front of our eyes with certain contrived truths scribbled on it. They place the paper too close to our eyes to prevent us from seeing the mountain of lies they love to hide.

As the public grope in the dark about the essence of the ISRO espionage case, a re-evaluation of the case is imperative to see afresh why the espionage story cropped up. It is most essential to re-read the text of the ISRO espionage case through documents, facts and prudence, and not through the projection of individuals as the good, the bad, and the ugly!

Hence, this book. The book addresses the *how* and the *why* aspects, besides the *who* factor, against the backdrop of the new development – a criminal investigation by the CBI against seven Kerala Police officers and eleven IB officials. To those who have studied the case in detail, this is nothing more than an act of buffoonery staged by the caged parrot to fix a *persona non grata.*

When I first exposed that the CIA had masterminded the espionage story in my book, *Spies from Space: The ISRO Frame-up* (1998), many readers, including some senior journalists said I was having apophenia. Three years later, Brian Harvey, a former BBC correspondent, expressed the same thought in his book, *Russia in Space: The Failed Frontier?* Today, the apophenia I had in 1998 is accepted worldwide.

In this book, I am trying to address the question – *Why* did the CIA plant the espionage story and, more importantly, *what* prompted the CIA to mastermind the spy story sixteen months after Russia had decided not to transfer cryogenic technology to India, something the US wanted the Russian government to do?

The book details the reverse espionage and a clandestine move planned simultaneously to illegally transfer cryogenic rocket technology from Glavkosmos to ISRO, hoodwinking the US intelligence. It also revolves around how the CIA burst the operations using its moles in IB. Furthermore, the book exposes a bizarre and nerve-wracking reality that both IB, India's premier intelligence-gathering agency, and the CBI, India's premier investigating agency, are ghost organizations, are illegal and exist in a constitutional vacuum.

You read it right. I am quoting the legal status of IB and CBI from certain legally vetted documents by two high courts and the Supreme Court.

The experiences of the victims of the espionage case are based on long interviews with the victims, besides their diaries and notes of despair. They are presented in their most authentic form. I have only chipped off the non-dramatic time and space from their trauma-scapes.

Since the IB interrogators never revealed their identity to the accused, I am constrained to identify them as Mr A, Mr B and so on.

Fact is the soul of journalism. Fact, for me, is the best available version of the truth.

Through this book, I am riding on hard facts and truths, in search of the truth behind the ISRO espionage case – the truth everyone loves to hide. Truth is always stranger than fiction, especially in this case. The spy story that put to ridicule all our institutions refuses to die for one reason or the other, even twenty-seven years after it was first reported. And those who echo the facts and truths run the risk of being branded as traitors by the establishment, where the press also becomes a willing accomplice by suppressing its questioning spirit.

Part - I

Revisiting the Spy Case

1
A Historiography

The chain of events that pulled ISRO down from its soaring pride, hardly five days after the successful launch of PSLV-D 2, began at 4.15 p.m. on 20 October 1994, with the arrest of Mariam Rasheeda – a Maldivian woman, held up due to cancellation of many flights from India, following the outbreak of plague in six Indian states.

A case of overstaying (Crime No. 225/94) under Section 14 of the Foreigners Act, 1946 and paragraph 7 of the Foreigner's Order, 1948 was registered against her. But, the next day, *Desabhimani*, the Malayalam newspaper, essentially CPI (M)[1] mouthpiece, reported the arrest as the crackdown on a spy ring operating from ISRO, which the newspaper wrongly described as India's defence organisation.

The story took a diabolic turn with *Kerala Kaumudi*, another local newspaper, naming Raman Srivastava IPS, the then Inspector General (IG) (South Zone), as the kingpin of the spy ring. The media and politicians cried for his blood. But, the then Chief Minister K. Karunakaran ignored the mood of the public, creating a strong impression that he was shielding his blue-eyed cop.

Meanwhile, Kerala Police, as directed by IB, enlarged the spy ring beyond Mariam Rasheeda and registered a case of espionage[2] against Fauziya Hassan, another Maldivian woman;

1. CPI (M) – Communist Party of India (Marxist)
2. Crime No.246/94, under Sections 3, 4, and 5 of Indian Official secrets Act, 1923

K. Chandrasekhar, representative of the Russian space agency Glavkosmos; S. K. Sharma, a Bangalore-based labour contractor; and S. Nambi Narayanan and D. Sasikumaran, technocrats in ISRO. The cases were handed over to an SIT headed by Siby Mathews IPS, DIG in Crime Branch, on 15 November 1994.

On 2 December 1994, the cases were transferred to CBI, after Siby Mathews wrote a letter to DGP Kerala, stating that the cases be transferred to CBI since Kerala Police was ill-equipped to investigate the spy case.[3] CBI registered one more case against all the accused under the Prevention of Corruption Act, 1947.

At this juncture, a legal forum based at Kochi filed a PIL before the High Court of Kerala, seeking a direction to CBI to arrest Raman Srivastava and to remove him from service invoking article 311 of the Constitution of India. The court dismissed the PIL since "no court can direct the investigating agency to implicate one as an accused and arrest him."

A division bench dismissed an appeal moved by the legal forum on 13 January 1995, upholding the decision of the single bench but ruled, quoting IB records, that Srivastava had links with the spy ring. Srivastava was suspended the same day.

At the political front, the observation of the court triggered a coup led by K. Karunakaran's arch-rival A.K. Antony with the overt support of the press in Kerala that saw the exit of K. Karunakaran as Chief Minister, which eventually paved the way for his long political exile.

CBI, RAW, IB and Union Home Ministry filed a joint Special Leave Petition before the Supreme Court against the observations of the High Court. The court passed its orders on 5 April 1995, chiding

3. Crime No. 225/94 and 246/94 thenceforth became R.C 10(S) 94 and R.C 11(S) 94.

the High Court's interference with the cryptic comment, "We say no more."

Though the Chief Judicial Magistrate (CJM), Ernakulam had granted bail to all the accused in the espionage case on 19 January 1995, the two Maldivian women could not taste freedom for want of sureties.

On 14 November 1995, the CJM acquitted Mariam Rasheeda in the overstay case and observed Inspector Vijayan, who had arrested her. The inspector was chasing her "from the middle of October 1994, obstructing her from leaving India".

While under judicial custody, Mariam Rasheeda gave two separate interviews to *India Today* and *Savvy*. She told *India Today* that Vijayan and Sub-Inspector Thampi S. Durgadatt had tortured her. To *Savvy* (I interviewed her), she confided she was a victim of Vijayan's thwarted sexual advances. The interviews generated four defamation cases – three criminal and one civil.

After eighteen months of investigation, on 30 April 1996, CBI filed Closure Report before the CJM[4], terming the espionage case "false and baseless". On 2 May 1996, the CJM accepted the report and discharged all the accused.

Technically speaking, Fauziya Hassan was free to leave India. But Inspector Vijayan filed a defamation case against her over an interview given to Asianet TV, and Fauziya was remanded to judicial custody, again for want of sureties.

On 3 June 1996, CBI filed two confidential reports, one each to the Government of India and the Kerala government, listing out certain serious lapses on the part of IB officials and Kerala Police officers during the investigation of the espionage case. The reports demanded action by the respective governments.

---

4. Under Section 173(2) of CrPC

While Government of India sat on the report, Kerala government decided to circumvent the charges made against its police officers through a legal interpolation. On 27 June 1996, the newly-elected Left Democratic Front (LDF) government in Kerala issued a notification for further investigation in the spy case under Section 173(8) CrPC.

The accused and the CBI challenged the notification[5] before the High Court. The court ruled that the State government has no jurisdiction even to file a complaint before a court under the Indian Official Secrets Act, 1923. The order was challenged before the Supreme Court by the accused, CBI and Union Government since the High Court didn't quash the notification.

On 11 December 1996, Fauziya Hassan was discharged from the defamation case. But within a couple of hours, the Kerala government invoked National Security Act (NSA) against her. One year later, the government was forced to set her free, as the Act does not permit detention beyond twelve months. She then flew back to the Maldives, a free bird.

The story of Mariam Rasheeda also has a similar note. On 6 September 1997, the Magistrate Court in Thiruvananthapuram granted her unconditional bail in all the defamation cases. But Kerala government invoked National Security Act (NSA) against her and prevented her from leaving India even after she was acquitted of all the major charges levelled against her.

On 29 April 1998, the Supreme Court of India quashed the Kerala government notification for further investigation as "patently invalid and unsustainable in law". The Bench ripped the democratic facade of the elected Kerala government. "Even if we were to hold that the State Government had the requisite power and authority to issue the impugned notification, still the same

---

5. O.P. No.14248/1996-U

would be liable to be quashed on the ground of mala fide exercise of power."

Justice M.K. Mukherjee and Justice Syed Shah Mohammed Quadri then gave the judicial whack.

> *From the above facts and circumstances, we are constrained to say that the issuance of the impugned notification does not comport with the known pattern of a responsible government bound by rule of law. This is undoubtedly a matter of concern and consternation. We say no more.*

The very next day, the Kerala government revoked NSA and Mariam Rasheeda was free. Meanwhile, ISRO reinstated S. Nambi Narayanan and D. Sasikumaran, who were under deemed suspension, following their arrest. S. K. Sharma rebuilt his business. K. Chandrasekhar reopened his ties with Glavkosmos. And Raman Srivastava was reinstated, following an order by the Central Administrative Tribunal.

While the other accused persons and Raman Srivastava IPS chose not to seek legal remedies, S. Nambi Narayanan approached the NHRC in April 1999 claiming compensation from the Kerala government for the mental agony and torture he had suffered. On 14 March 2001, NHRC awarded an interim compensation of ten lakh rupees and asked the State to pay damages. Kerala government moved to High Court, challenging the order.

In 2003, Nambi Narayanan filed a suit[6] before the sub-court, Thiruvananthapuram, seeking damages to the tune of one crore. His suit was against certain officials in both Kerala Police and IB, and Kerala government and Union government. The Kerala

6. O.S. No. 370/2003

government offered him 1.3 crore for an out-of-court settlement.[7] Nambi Narayanan withdrew the suit, unconditionally, agreeing to have no further claim against any of the defendants and that "no personal liability can be fixed on the officials accused of falsely implicating him."

In 2010, I moved a Public Interest Litigation (PIL) before the High Court [W.P. (C) No. 8080] seeking direction to Kerala government to take action on a file pending with the government since 12 December 1996 with a noting by the then Chief Minister E.K. Nayanar that action against the 'erring' police officers, as required by CBI, could be considered after the Supreme Court order in the further investigation case. Though the Supreme Court had passed its order quashing the notification for further investigation on 29 April 1998, the successive State governments sat on the noting of E.K. Nayanar for fourteen years. On 29 June 2011, Kerala government decided not to take any disciplinary action against the (erring) police officers and the High Court disposed of my O.P.

Aggrieved by the decision of the State government, Nambi Narayanan approached the High Court[8] to quash the government order. On 20 October 2014, the court quashed the government order and remitted back the matter to the government for consideration and passing further orders within three months. The court made it clear – "the course of action to be taken in the matter is left open to be decided by the government. Suffice to say that it should not be namesake, making administration of justice a mockery."

Siby Mathews moved an appeal against the order[9], and a Division Bench on 4 March 2015 set aside the judgment of the Single Bench

---

7. GO (MS) No 203/2019 Home, dated 27 December 2019
8. W.P. (C) 30918 of 2012
9. WA.NO. 1863 OF 2014

because "the direction to remit the matter back to the government will be a futile exercise and requires to be set aside... when the decision has been taken not to proceed further with any disciplinary action."

S. Nambi Narayanan then approached the Supreme Court.

On 14 September 2018, a three-member bench headed by Chief Justice Dipak Misra awarded fifty lakh rupees as compensation to S. Nambi Narayanan to be paid by the Kerala government. Besides, the court constituted a committee headed by D.K. Jain, a former Supreme Court judge, to "find out the means to take appropriate steps against the erring police officials."

The Committee submitted its report after nearly two-and-a-half years and the Supreme Court, on 15 April 2021, ordered CBI to look into the report. Accordingly, CBI registered an FIR against certain Kerala Police officers for allegedly framing S. Nambi Narayanan on false charges in the ISRO espionage case.

On 1 May 2021, the Delhi unit of CBI filed an FIR against seven Kerala Police officers and eleven IB officers before the CJM, Thiruvananthapuram, and charged them with conspiracy, framing of false evidence, and illegal custody of S. Nambi Narayanan. This is where the ISRO espionage case rests now.

After nearly twenty-seven years of heat and dust, the ISRO espionage case crafted by CIA and planted by its moles in IB through Kerala Police and sensationalized by the media now revolves around the arrest and torture of one person – S. Nambi Narayanan.

2

CBI Reloaded

1 May 2021

The CBI, India's premier investigating agency, proved what Karl Marx wrote in 1852. "History repeats itself, first as tragedy, second as farce."

In the fifth paragraph of its confidential report sent to the Chief Secretary, Government of Kerala[10] listing out the serious lapses on the part of certain officers in Kerala Police, CBI accused the Kerala Police for not registering the espionage case much earlier (than 13 November 1994).

> *Despite the lingering suspicions about the conduct of Rasheeda and Fauziya harboured by Kerala Police and the IB officials, and the fact that the local press was playing up the issue and even the name of Raman Srivastava, IGP, was also being linked up with this episode, no immediate steps were taken by the Kerala Police to register a case under the Official Secrets Act and effect the arrest of accused persons.*

The history was a tragedy because through this statement, CBI paraded its ignorance of Section 13 (3) and (5) of the Indian Official Secrets Act (IOS Act), 1923 that prevents either Kerala Police or CBI

10. Letter No. 2783/3/11(S) 94—SIUV/SIC, dated 3 June 1996

from registering or investigating a case under the Act without a complaint in writing by the appropriate government (in the case of ISRO, it is the Central government) reaching the competent Magistrate, who can take cognizance of the offence.

Twenty-five years later, when the same CBI filed the FIR[11] against eighteen persons, including seven officers in Kerala Police, before the CJM, Thiruvananthapuram, for arresting S. Nambi Narayanan in the ISRO espionage case under the Indian Officials Secrets Act, 1923, it allowed history to repeat as farce.

The accused IB officers are – Raveendran Nair, R.B. Sreekumar, Mathew John, C.R.R. Nair, K.V. Thomas, P.S. Jayaprakash, G.S. Nair, John Punnan, Baby, Dinta Mathiyas and V.K. Maini. The accused police officers are – S. Vijayan, Thampi S. Durgadatt, V.R. Rajeevan, Siby Mathews, G. Baburaj, S. Jogesh and K.K. Joshua.

All the accused are charged with ten crimes under the Indian Penal Code (IPC): 120- B (Criminal conspiracy); 167 (Public servant framing an incorrect document with intent to cause injury); 218 (Public servant framing incorrect record or writing with intent to save person from punishment or property from forfeiture); 330 (Voluntarily causing hurt to extort confession, or to compel restoration of property); 323 (Punishment for voluntarily causing hurt); 195 (Giving or fabricating false evidence with intent to procure conviction of offence punishable with imprisonment for life or imprisonment); 348 (Wrongful confinement to extort confession, or compel restoration of property); 365 (Kidnapping or abducting with intent secretly and wrongfully to confine person); 477A (Falsification of accounts) and 506 (Punishment for criminal intimidation).

Since the CBI has charged the accused with IPC 365, it implies certain Kerala Police officers named in the FIR had abducted

11. RC/050/2021/S0007 of SC-II Delhi Police Station, dated 1/5/2021

S. Nambi Narayanan before he was illegally arrested and tortured. But this is what Nambi Narayanan had told me about his arrest when I interviewed him for *Society* magazine[12]. "On 30 November, I couldn't go to the office due to health problems. At 3.30 p.m., some men dressed in plain clothes escorted me to the local police station. They didn't arrest me, nor did they give me the impression that I was under arrest."

On the face of it, it seems that the CBI has included everyone involved in the investigation of the ISRO espionage case in the FIR. But a deeper look into it would reveal something else.

The basis of the FIR is the report of the D.K. Jain Committee constituted by the Supreme Court of India on 14 September 2018. It was to "find out ways and means to take appropriate steps against the erring officials" on the basis that the "authorities that have been responsible to cause such kind of harrowing effect on the mind of the appellant *(Nambi Narayanan)* should face the legal consequences."[13]

The Jain Committee submitted its report two-and-a-half years after it was formed. Within days of the Committee submitting its report, the Central Government, on 5 April 2021, moved to the top court seeking urgent hearing and consideration of the panel's report terming it as a national issue.

A bench led by A.M. Khanwilkar said the report concerned a "serious matter" that warrants a CBI probe and "requires thorough probe". The Court also barred the public circulation of the contents of the report.

The FIR was based on the D.K. Jain Committee Report. The Jain Committee was created by an order of the Supreme Court; the

12. June, 1995
13. Para 40 of the Supreme Court Judgment in Civil Appeal Nos. 6637-6638 of 2018

order was issued while allowing a civil appeal by Nambi Narayanan; and Nambi Narayanan's case was for legal action against the erring Kerala Police officers.

If that's the case, how could CBI name the IB officers in the FIR?

Nambi Narayanan's case before the Supreme Court was clearly to not take any legal action against the IB officials. That's because the genesis of his case is a Kerala Government order dated 29 June 2011 that decided not to take any action against the erring Kerala Police officers. The order was submitted before Kerala High Court in a PIL[14], seeking directions to the State of Kerala to pass appropriate orders and take necessary action against the erring police officers based on the report filed by CBI on 3 June 1996. It is against this government order that Nambi Narayanan moved to court, which was finally decided by the Supreme Court in his favour on 14 September 2018.

I had filed the PIL before the High Court on 7 March 2010. My petition was not specifically against officers in Kerala Police or IB. It was a writ of Mandamus seeking direction to the State government to take action on the file[15], demanding action against the erring Kerala police officers[16].

Even after the then chief minister had given his assent to a note by the then chief secretary that "Decision may be taken on receipt of the Supreme Court judgment" on 12 December 1997, the file was kept in the cold storage for twelve years. Though the apex court had passed its judgment on 29 April 1998 and put on record that "from the above facts and circumstances, we are constrained to say that

14. W.P. (C) No. 8080 of 2010
15. 66412/SSA3/97/Home that originated with CBI filing its Confidential Report vide Letter No. 2783/3/11(S) 94—SIUV/SIC, dated 3 June 1996
16. Reported in paragraphs 11 and 12 of the Supreme Court Judgment in Civil Appeal Nos. 6637-6638 of 2018.

the issuance of the impugned notification (for further investigation of the espionage case by Kerala Police)does not comport with the known pattern of a responsible government bound by rule of law. This is undoubtedly a matter of concern and consternation. We say no more."

After my petition was disposed of in 2011, Nambi Narayanan moved the High Court through WP (C) No. 30918 of 2012 (L) and made the State of Kerala, Home Secretary of Kerala government, CBI, Siby Mathews, K.K. Joshua and S. Vijayan as respondents 1 to 6. His prayer was to quash the Government Order[17] that decided not to take any action against Siby Mathews, K.K. Joshua, and S. Vijayan.

The court quashed the government order and remitted the matter back to the government "for reconsideration and for issuing formal orders".

Siby Mathews challenged the order on which a Division Bench passed judgment on 4 March 2015. "The only question before the government was whether any disciplinary action was to be initiated against the officers who were members of the Special Investigation Team which conducted the investigation for some days and thereafter reported that the matter required to be investigated by the CBI. The factual finding submitted by the CBI on 3 June 1996 in the matter could only be treated as an opinion expressed by the CBI which may be considered by the government."

It was this order that Nambi Narayanan had challenged before the Supreme Court. He didn't pray for compensation since he was fighting a case for compensation to the tune of one crore rupees in a sub-court in Thiruvananthapuram.

If the court aimed to see what steps could be taken against the erring officials of Kerala Police – which is clear in the delivered

17. (RT) No. 1923/2011/Home dated 29/6/2011

judgment and constituting the D.K. Jain Committee – why did CBI include names of the IB officers in the FIR?

It can only be presumed that the CBI got the names from the D.K. Jain Committee Report since the Supreme Court, through its order on 15 April 2021, has made it clear – "This report shall not be made public. In other words, the report is not for public circulation. It can be used by the CBI during further enquiry process that is required to be undertaken by the CBI as recommended in the report."

Again, there is nothing in the order of the Supreme Court to establish that the court had contemplated a comprehensive enquiry into all factors connected with the spy scandal. For instance, the court didn't order compensation to the other five accused in the ISRO espionage case. The court in no part of its forty-one paragraph-judgment raised any concern for the accused, except for Nambi Narayanan.[18]

Let us analyze the spirit of the FIR. If the FIR is about torturing Nambi Narayanan; even Nambi Narayanan has no case that anyone from Kerala Police had tortured him.

At the same time, it is a fact that the CBI sleuths had tortured all the six accused, including Nambi Narayanan, brutally (as is evident from the statements of fellow accused D. Sasikumaran) till he confided to the CBI top brass about a partially-succeeded reverse espionage to transfer the cryogenic technology from Glavkosmos to ISRO, as desired by ISRO top brass, in which he had a lead role to play, and the CBI got it confirmed.

If the CBI is investigating the torture inflicted on S. Nambi Narayanan, then it has to book the CBI team members who had investigated the espionage case.

---

18. Paragraphs 16, 17, 18, 19, 31, 29, and 40 of the judgment

If the FIR is about fabricating the spy case, you can't blame Siby Mathews, since the espionage case was registered on 13 November 1994, two days before the case was transferred to SIT under him.

It leaves three Kerala Police officers – S. Vijayan, Thampi S. Durgadatt and V. R. Rajeevan – against whom the CBI could have moved. But the FIR lists the names of eighteen persons. Paragraph eight of the FIR reads, "After conducting the enquiry, the Committee submitted its report on 25.3.2021 before the Hon'ble Supreme Court. In the report, the Committee has pointed out apparent involvement of the following officials in falsely implicating Shri S. Nambi Narayanan."

It means the CBI had taken the names from the D.K. Jain Committee report without doing any research of its own. In the process, it included the name of V.R. Rajeevan, the then Commissioner of Police, Thiruvananthapuram, who had died in 2019, two years before the D.K. Jain Committee submitted its report. The credit of naming a dead person as an accused, therefore, should go jointly to the D.K. Jain Committee and CBI.

If the FIR is about the illegal arrest and custody of S. Nambi Narayanan by the Kerala Police officers, the same applies to the CBI officers also who kept Nambi Narayanan under their custody. The illegality of the arrest in the espionage case arises not because the case was later found to be false and baseless. In that case, every accused person arrested but later discharged or acquitted for want of evidence, anywhere in India, should get the same justice that the Supreme Court had delivered in favour of S. Nambi Narayanan.

The arrest of S. Nambi Narayanan and other five persons in the espionage case becomes illegal because the Kerala Police had invoked Sections 3, 4 and 5 of the IOS Act, 1923, which they were not empowered to invoke. According to Section 13 (3) of the IOS Act, "no court shall take cognizance of any offence under this Act unless upon complaint made by order of, or under authority from, the appropriate government or some officer empowered by the appropriate government on this behalf." The appropriate government, as per Section 13(5) of the Act, is the Central government in the case of ISRO. Resultantly, the ISRO spy case should have originated through a complaint filed by the Central government to the competent Magistrate; and not through a police FIR under Section 154 of Code of Criminal Procedure (CrPC).

By that logic, if the custody of Nambi Narayanan under the IOS Act by Kerala Police was illegal, his custody under CBI was also illegal. And for the same reason, all the activities, right from the registration of the espionage case, were illegal.

- On 13 November 1994, Kerala Police registered Crime No. 246/94, better known as the ISRO spy case, under Sections 3, 4, and 5 of the IOS Act. The act of Kerala Police officers, who were acting under the dictation of IB, was illegal since it violated Section 13(3) and (5) of the IOS Act. Thus, the very genesis of the espionage case was illegal and hence, void and invalid.
- On 15 November 1994, Crime No. 246/94 was transferred to an SIT of Kerala Police. The act was invalid for the same reason.
- Crime No 246/94 was transferred to CBI on 4 December 1994. The act was invalid for the same reason.
- CBI, after 18 months of investigation, submitted a Closure Report under Section 173(2) CrPC to CJM, Ernakulam. The act was invalid for the same reason.
- CJM accepted the report that concluded the case was "false and baseless" and discharged all the six accused. The action of CJM was illegal and invalid since there was no complaint from ISRO to the competent Magistrate at any point in time.
- While the CBI investigation was progressing, two learned judges

of the High Court of Kerala passed orders castigating CBI and made certain observations that triggered a political coup in Kerala, besides casting a shadow over the reputation of an IG of Police, fully knowing that the court had no legal authority over the case at that stage of the investigation. The judges who dared to trespass into the forbidden area, however, didn't notice that the very genesis of Crime No. 246/94 was illegal.

- On 27 June 1996, the Kerala Government issued a notice for further investigation of Crime No. 246/94 under Section 173(8) of CrPC. The notification, besides being illegal and invalid for many reasons, was invalid because the genesis of 246/94 was illegal.
- On 27 November 1996, a Division Bench of the High Court of Kerala passed its orders on a bunch of writs challenging the notification. The Bench declared that the State police have no right to further investigate the case since the police cannot approach any court in India with that report because of the application of Section 13(3) of the IOS Act. But the court didn't quash the entire proceedings, including the investigations conducted by Kerala Police and CBI, citing the same reason. It also didn't quash the judicial act of the Magistrate who accepted the CBI report, citing the same Section 13(3).
- On 29 April 1998, the Supreme Court quashed the further investigation notification of Kerala Government, but didn't put on record that the case was bad in law, right from its genesis.

If the FIR is about some conspiracy in framing S. Nambi Narayanan, the CBI needs a lot of explanation since the spy case was not to fix Nambi Narayanan or, for that matter, any single individual; but to derail ISRO's space trajectory and sabotage India's cryogenic dreams. The real target and the victim of the espionage case, then and now, is ISRO; the framing of one Nambi Narayanan or all was only incidental, and the damage caused to one or all was only collateral.

There was indeed a conspiracy. It was an international conspiracy fabricated by the CIA. The officials of Kerala Police and IB included in the FIR, at the most, were pawns used by some top brass in IB, who worked as trusted moles of the CIA. But their names are not in the FIR.

Chronology of events testify that the espionage story, as we know today, was aired after M.K. Dhar, then Joint Director of IB, air-dashed to Thiruvananthapuram in the first week of November 1994 and took command of the operations.

Proof for this is the CBI's Confidential Report[19] addressed to the Secretary, Ministry of Home Affairs, and Government of India. Paragraph 25 of the report reads:

> *C.M. Raveendran, the then DD, SIB, Bombay, who was associated with the interrogation of Mariam Rasheeda has stated that till he was in Thiruvananthapuram interrogating accused Rasheeda, no espionage angle came to his notice. He had prepared a report in this regard and submitted it to John Mathew, JD, IB.*

Similarly, records with the Kerala High Court show "P.S. Jayaprakash, Assistant Central Intelligence Officer Grade-I of the S.I.B., Kochi, was part of the team that was helping the Kerala Police to investigate the case from 04.11.1994 to 30.11.1994, and thereafter, he left the team." He did not take part in any manner in the interrogation or arrest of Nambi Narayanan since Nambi Narayanan was arrested on 30 November 1994, the day he had left

19. Letter No. 2782/3/11(S) 94—SIUV/SIC, dated 3 June 1996

the investigation team. He had not even met Nambi Narayanan. Interestingly, both C.M. Raveendran and P.S. Jayaprakash are accused in the FIR filed by CBI, while M.K. Dhar is not an accused.

Rattan Sehgal, then Additional Director of IB was put under house arrest in December 1996 because he had "nine unauthorised and clandestine" meetings with the US Embassy station chief of the CIA, Timothy Long, and his deputy Susan Brown between 19 September and 31 October 1996, in Sehgal's Bharati Nagar residence and the parking lot of Ambassador Hotel in Delhi. On 18 September, he received a large packet from Ms August, the former deputy station chief of the CIA, outside Ambassador Hotel.

On 19 November 1996, at a meeting with the Union Home Secretary Padmanabhaiah, Arun Bhagat, the Director of IB stated, "An analysis of the evidence shows that Sehgal was not working for the CIA but was probably being cultivated by the Americans." [20]

Curiously, IB forwarded a letter to the Ministry of Home Affairs on 18 November 1996, in which the agency clearly stated that "the officer (Rattan Sehgal) was not facing any vigilance/ departmental enquiry and therefore his request for voluntary retirement may be accepted."

A tweet by N.K. Sood, a former RAW top brass on 18 July 2019, adds a new dimension as to how the government allowed the big fish to escape the legal net.

> *Rattan Sehgal, Addl Director, IB was caught passing on sensitive documents to CIA in 96. (He) was allowed to resign (and) go to the USA. He also falsely implicated Nambi Narayanan in the infamous ISRO spy case.*

Why then did Rattan Sehgal's name not appear in the FIR registered by CBI?

---

20. *India Today,* 15 March 1997

CBI's confidential report[21] tells volumes about the role of D.C. Pathak, the then Director of IB, in building the spy story.

- The Director of Intelligence Bureau (DIB) issued several UO (unofficial) notes to the Cabinet Secretary, Home Minister, Principal Secretary to Prime Minister, Home Secretary, and other high functionaries of the Government of India in this regard.
- In his UO Note[22] dated 28 November 1994, Pathak mentioned that the DGP, Kerala, has to be advised immediately to bring Raman Srivastava, IG of Police, in the ambit of the case.

In a subsequent UO note, dated 1 December 1994, D.C. Pathak stated that Srivastava had emerged as the most important member of the inner group of the spy ring without giving any hint about the evidence available on record against Srivastava. This is evident from the UO Note[23] in which the DIB observes that "Raman Srivastava, IGP, Thiruvananthapuram is being examined and his movements etc. are being checked up."

- In other words, twenty-one days after D.C. Pathak had concluded that Raman Srivastava was an important member of the inner group of the spy ring, IB was still examining his movements.
- D.C. Pathak sent several UO notes to important functionaries, without realizing that those notes would be treated as authentic and having been sent after careful verification and consequences.

---

21. Letter No. 2782/3/11(S) 94—SIU V/SIC, dated 3 June 1996, addressed to the Secretary, Ministry of Home Affairs, Government of India
22. No. 9/ESP (U)/94 (3)-11-309 dated 28 November 1995, D.C.
23. No. 334/DIB/DESP/94 dated 22 December 1994

- With regards to the role of Managing Partner of Machine Tools Aid and Reconditioning (MTAR) Ravindra Reddy, Director of Intelligence Bureau (DIB) in the aforesaid note further went on to say that "the allegation that one MTAR Ravindra Reddy, a scientist of ISRO, was closely related to the CM of Andhra Pradesh, and that he has business dealings with Prabhakar Rao has not been substantiated. Prima facie, there is nothing against this Ravindra Reddy in this case."
- It is crystal clear that DIB first issued UO notes to the highest functionaries in the Government of India indicating the involvement of Raman Srivastava, MTAR Ravindra Reddy and others, and subsequently negated his version (given in the earlier notes).
- It is also important to note that there is no person called MTAR Ravindra Reddy. It is P. Ravindra Reddy, MTAR, located at Balangar, Hyderabad. He was never an ISRO scientist.
- The investigation further disclosed that Prabhakar Rao s/o Narasimha Rao, Prime Minister of India, had no business dealings with Ravindra Reddy. Reddy was examined in this regard and he denied having any business dealings with Prabhakar Rao.

In his UO Note[24], D.C. Pathak tells that he had requested the DGP, Kerala, to enlarge the structure of the case registered against Mariam Rasheeda and Fauziya Hassan under Sections 3, 4, and 5 of the IOS Act.

▼

It is important to note that D. Sasikumaran, S. Nambi Narayanan, K. Chandrasekhar and S.K. Sharma were arrested and made accused

24. No.303/DIB/DESP/94 dated 21 November 1994

in the espionage case following D.C. Pathak's request to expand the scope of the espionage case.

Besides, D.C. Pathak was primarily responsible for giving wrong information to the Chairman of ISRO. That silenced ISRO from coming out with the factual information that ISRO didn't have the cryogenic technology in 1994 and therefore, the spy story was absurd. If the ISRO Chairman had shown the integrity and honesty expected of his office, the espionage story would have ended on day one. ISRO Chairman K. Kasturirangan didn't do it because D.C. Pathak had told him over the phone that incriminating documents had been seized from the scientists and that defence secrets were now with IB. Chairman ISRO feared whether he too would be branded a spy if he dared to tell the truth.

That raises another question. Why didn't CBI include D.C. Pathak's name in the FIR registered before the CJM, Thiruvananthapuram?

The present exercise of CBI is not to bring to light the conspiracy leading to the ISRO espionage case. CBI knows pretty well that the factors leading to the espionage case would ultimately lead CBI to the hitherto undisclosed reverse espionage and its fallout. Neither the Union government nor the Supreme Court and CBI want it to happen. The whole intention of this staged study is to bury the possibilities of the real facts behind the espionage case reaching the public domain – who all conspired, who all were instrumental in planting it, why it was planted and how it was planted.

The FIR, to put it mildly, is an attempt to hide the obvious. To pull the wool over real facts behind the ISRO espionage case, and to frame-up a *persona non grata*.

▼

Reacting to the new FIR filed by CBI, S. Nambi Narayanan said the country suffered badly due to the case. "The cryogenic project (of ISRO) was delayed. Let conspiracy come out."[25]

It is Nambi Narayanan's ploy. He has been playing with it for some years now. He would never approach any court in India for anything other than to redress his grievances. He would never pray to any court for a judicial probe to bring out the whole facts surrounding the ISRO espionage case because it would put him and many leading figures in ISRO in the soup. At the same time, he presents himself as the messiah of social justice before the media, trying his best to bring to the public domain every piece of information regarding the ISRO frame up.

Few believe him when Nambi Narayanan tells "let conspiracy come out", as he means the conspiracy that led to his arrest *only*. He doesn't want the conspiracy of the CIA, planted through certain top brass in IB, to come out.

In my opinion, the CBI investigation has three objectives:

- One is to project the ISRO spy case as the sad story of framing up S. Nambi Narayanan, a scientist who would have, but for his illegal arrest and torture, taken ISRO to new orbits in rocketry.
- The second one aims to hide the unpleasant facts of a reverse espionage to illegally bring the cryogenic rocket technology from Glavkosmos to ISRO, hoodwinking the hawkish eyes of the CIA and to retell the absurd spy story in an even more absurd manner as one created by ISI and Pakistan to sabotage India's cryogenic dreams – a narrative that has the inbuilt catharsis of enemy-bashing and patriotism.
- The third is to fix R.B. Sreekumar, a persona non grata, for his arrogance and impudence to file an affidavit before Nanavati-

25. *https://www.hindustantimes.com,* 25 June 2021

Mehta Commission and to make a presentation to James Michael Lyngdoh, the then Chief Election Commissioner of India, alleging the dubious role of law and order in the Godhra carnage (2002) and subsequent riots, when he was the Additional DGP in Gujarat.

All the three intentions of the reloaded CBI showed their ugly faces on 29 July 2021 when it aired brazen lies before the Kerala High Court while opposing the anticipatory bail application moved by R.B. Sreekumar.

Opposing the bail, Additional Solicitor General S.V. Raju, appearing for CBI, argued that the case was a serious matter involving national security. The case was foisted on the two leading scientists at the behest of ISI. The CBI strongly believed that Pakistan was involved in the case. It was done to derail the ISRO programme to develop a cryogenic engine. [26]

In 1994, IB and Kerala Police told us that ISRO was a defence organization and the espionage case was about selling India's cryogenic missile technology to Pakistan and painted two former ISRO-technocrats as spies who sold the nation's pride to Pakistan, our eternal enemy. The fact is that ISRO was and is not a defence organization. There is nothing like cryogenic missile technology anywhere in use in the world, and ISRO didn't have cryogenic rocket technology in 1994.

Twenty-seven years later, the same CBI that had investigated the espionage case for eighteen months and didn't find anybody's hand, including that of Pakistan, is now saying that R.B. Sreekumar is an ISI man. And, the arrest of ISRO-technocrats was to sabotage ISRO's programme to develop the cryogenic engine, as desired by

---

26. *The Hindu*, 29 July 2021

Pakistan, even as an investigation under a new FIR, registered on 1 May 2021, is in infancy and the CBI sleuths are yet to interrogate any of the accused!

Why didn't the CBI team that investigated the espionage case for 18 months from December 1994 see this hand of ISI and Pakistan which the new CBI team could read from nowhere?

Which of the two teams of the CBI, the premier investigating agency of India, is a damp squib? The first one or the new one?

More importantly, why does S. Nambi Narayanan, a key figure in the failed reverse espionage (from Glavkosmos to ISRO in 1994), remain silent?

Is this what he had been looking for all these years? While practising legal jugglery with one hand and pampering the media, that once tortured him by taking them to the orbit of lies through camouflaged trajectories, with the other hand. Was he hoping that some State agency would come, one day, to pull the wool over the failed reverse espionage, in which he had a lead role to play, and weave contrived stories of patriotism and the green-eyed enemy country around the ruins of the failed espionage?

Something the reloaded CBI team is unabashedly doing?

Meanwhile, the Kerala High Court while granting bail to four of the accused, including R.B. Sreekumar, who approached the court, recorded on 13 August 2021 – "There is not even a scintilla of evidence regarding the petitioners being influenced by any foreign power to induce them to hatch a conspiracy to falsely implicate the scientists of the ISRO to stall the activities of the ISRO concerning the development of Cryogenic Engine."

This statement of the order is pertinent in the context of the new investigation by the new team of CBI that presented before the court a false narrative about the involvement of ISI and Pakistan even before the investigation had begun. Additional Solicitor General

S.V. Raju, appearing for the CBI, didn't mention anything about the reverse espionage in which the ISRO top brass and S. Nambi Narayanan had lead roles. It is naïve to think CBI is oblivious of reverse espionage; something every agency of the State, including the CBI and ISRO, wants to hide.

It is stated with absolute certainty that the first CBI team that investigated the espionage case had full knowledge about the failed reverse espionage; a critical piece of information divulged to the CBI sleuths by S. Nambi Narayanan during interrogation. After the CBI top brass got it confirmed by the ISRO top brass, the interrogators stopped torturing the accused, redirected the investigation to disprove the absurd espionage theory aired by IB and Kerala Police, and concluded, applying the art of alibi, that the charges of espionage were false.

Facts are hacked and buried surreptitiously. The caged parrot is being tutored to quaver lies even before the courts of law. The stage is set for a new episode of the ISRO espionage case; this time with patriotic rhetoric and war cry against the eternal enemy.

3

A Can of Worms

27 January 2019

"More than two decades ago, a hardworking and patriotic ISRO scientist Nambi Narayanan was implicated in a false case, just because a few United Democratic Front (UDF) leaders were settling political scores. Imagine, for their politics, they damaged national interest, troubled a scientist." Prime Minister Narendra Modi made this statement while addressing a rally at Thrissur in Kerala. He was making a factually incorrect statement to the nation. The political coup in 1995 by the now-dead Antony Group in the Congress Party in Kerala to oust K. Karunakaran as Chief Minister was a political fallout of the ISRO espionage case, and not vice versa.

Narendra Modi's statement is the latest in a series of factually incorrect statements, postulates, and conclusions on and about the super sensational spy case that hit the headlines in 1994. More importantly, it is an interesting piece of journalism that refuses to die for one reason or the other, even after twenty-seven years.

What was the ISRO espionage case all about?

Was it a simple case of overstay of a Maldivian woman painted in sinister colours by both the press and police in Kerala?

Or the outcome of the sexual frustration of a Circle Inspector, who thought he had an easy game in hand?

Was it the wrath of the editor of a Malayalam newspaper against a high-profile IG and a self-styled king-maker of Indian politics?

Was it a meticulously-planned international commercial conspiracy by the CIA to deny India a share of the multi-billion dollar space market?

Or was it a mixture of all these with different agencies adding layers to the spy case at different points in time, aiming different targets?

When I first reported in 1998 that the ISRO spy case, contrary to what we have been made to believe, was basically and fundamentally a commercial detonator fabricated by the CIA and planted by its moles in IB, piggybacking on Kerala Police and the press in Kerala, not many believed it. The tables have turned since then. The CIA wanted to make sure that India does not get cryogenic rocket technology from Russia. The US administration feared it would capacitate ISRO to launch satellites into the geostationary orbit at 35, 786 km on commercial basis and seize a sizeable portion of the global space market. The numbers that follow speak for themselves, justifying the US insecurity.

With a projection of $77 billion by 1997, when the ISRO-Glavkosmos agreement was signed in 1991, the commercial prospect of the space market crossed $360 billion in 2018, and is expected to touch $558 billion by 2026, recording a growth of 5.6%. The American investment bank Morgan Stanley predicts, it "could nearly double, triple, or quintuple in size, growing to anywhere from 600 billion US Dollars to 1.75 trillion by 2040."

US anxiety may be justifiable from the American angle since a larger chunk of the space market was and is being appropriated by the US space players. ISRO, with its payload price tentatively fixed at less than half the price charged by the US launch vehicles, anticipated to pocket nearly 50% of the $300 billion space market by 2010.

But all the commercial calculations of ISRO went awry and all the apprehensions of America were effectively addressed once the US administration could arm-twist Russia and get the agreement to transfer cryogenic technology to ISRO cancelled in July 1993.

Facts being so, what could have prompted the CIA to plant an absurd spy case, sixteen months *after* the US administration had succeeded in stopping the transfer of Russian Cryogenic technology to India and ambushed India's space dreams?

A re-reading of the chronology of events that followed ISRO and Glavkosmos signing the agreement on 18 January 1991 for buying three cryogenic stages and for the transfer of cryogenic rocket technology to ISRO for 235 crore rupees is important to understand why the spy case came from nowhere with a deafening bang.

- Within a few months after the ISRO-Glavkosmos agreement was inked, the US State Secretary sent a letter to his Soviet counterpart expressing America's displeasure over the agreement.
- Meanwhile, the Soviet Union collapsed. Russia agreed to scrap the technology transfer at a meeting between Bill Clinton and Boris Yeltsin in April 1993 in Vancouver. On 20 July 1993, Russia cancelled the agreement, invoking *force majeure*.
- A modified agreement was signed between ISRO and Glavkosmos in January 1994. The agreement didn't have the crucial technology transfer segment. Russia had fully protected the US commercial interest.

Why did the CIA then plant a spy story sixteen months later?

Scrutiny of certain clandestine operations between Glavkosmos and ISRO between 4 March 1992 and 17 July 1994 explains what prompted the CIA to plant the ISRO espionage story. It also gives a clue why CBI, ISRO, the scientific community and Nambi Narayanan do not want the real facts behind the ISRO espionage case to reach the public domain.

How many of us know that the spy case was fabricated by the CIA to bring to sub-zero ISRO's partially succeeded reverse espionage – an illegal act done clandestinely, to transfer the cryogenic rocket technology from Glavkosmos to ISRO, hoodwinking the hawkish eyes of the US, after the agreement for the transfer of technology was cancelled?

How many of us know that reverse espionage was attempted with the connivance of ISRO management and a powerful group in Glavkosmos that acted against the will of the Russian government with S. Nambi Narayanan and D. Sasikumaran as the lead players in it?

How many of us know that the spy case, a technological nonsense, was aired by the CIA with the full confidence that neither ISRO nor Space Commission members would open their mouth to burst the spy ring theory? Because then, they would be opening a can of worms.

And the ISRO espionage case is a can of worms no one wants to open.

▼

The learned judges of the Supreme Court who endorsed the CBI findings that the espionage case was "false and baseless" on 29 April 1998 never asked who planted the spy case in the first place. Nor did they raise any questions on the hows and whys of the false case.

The scientist community – including Prof Satish Dhawan, Prof U.R. Rao, Prof Yashpal, Prof R. Narasimha and Prof

S. Chandrasekhar – and former bureaucrat T.N. Seshan wrote an open letter on 26 December 1996, wherein it is said, "the 'espionage' case reveals that the country's space programme, or for that matter other strategic programmes, may no longer be immune to outside interference." Despite saying that, it did not demand a comprehensive enquiry to bring out the facts holed up in the opaque layers that made up the espionage story.

The signatories hint at some foreign agency behind the spy case. They know it was to sabotage India's space programme and even apprehend outside interference detrimental to ISRO in the future. Yet, they wouldn't name the foreign agency and wouldn't even hint at why it was done. It is not fair to think that the signatories, some of them being Space Commission members from ISRO, were beating around the bush.

ISRO, the real victim of the espionage case, doesn't want the factors that led to the espionage story to reach the public domain since such an exercise would puncture its credentials as the country's premier space research organization with an annual budget of 13,949 crore (in 2021).

The Central government could have ordered for a Judicial Commission to look into the whole issue from all possible angles, but it didn't. The government knows that there are skeletons in the closet, and doesn't want its citizens to see it. It believes that pseudo patriotism is the panacea for all known and unknown ills and falls.

S. Nambi Narayanan, who has approached the courts in India more than ten times, did not ask for a comprehensive judicial enquiry, though he knew who did it and why it was done.

Those who actually know the *who, how and why* of this case, wouldn't dare to speak the truth.

Those who ought to have brought the facts before the public were happy airing stories of the espionage soap opera that had nothing to do with the matter they were reporting. More recently, they have been indulging in an easy game of storytelling by transposing the characters whereby the old villains have become the new heroes and the old heroes have become the new villains. So they have cast a new hero, S. Nambi Narayanan, an old 'spy'; and a new villain, Siby Mathews, the old hero. Remember, the very same Siby Mathews got the President's Police Medal for Meritorious Service for his exemplary work in the ISRO espionage case as the SIT leader in 1998.

One wonders why the Supreme Court didn't order for a judicial probe to bring out the facts, despite having the power and authority to do so. Instead, it constituted a committee to decide what action could be taken against three or four Kerala Police officials who had Nambi Narayanan under custody only for five days; against whom Nambi has no case of torture.

Contrary to what we are being made to believe in recent times by the Supreme Court, the Prime Minister and the media, the ISRO espionage case was not all about S. Nambi Narayanan and the torture inflicted on him. There are five more accused and discharged persons.

Part - II

Plot and Counter-Plot

4

Male Ego is Hurt

8 October 1994

Mariam Rasheeda, a Maldivian citizen with a passport[27] met Inspector S. Vijayan of the Foreigners Section in Thiruvananthapuram City Police Commissioner's Office around 11.30 a.m., seeking his official help to get her to stay in India extended beyond 17 October.

The Maldivians need no visa to stay in India.[28] Mariam Rasheeda made three visits to India in 1994. The first visit was to Thiruvananthapuram on 2 June 1994. She returned seven days later. She came to Thiruvananthapuram again on 20 June and returned after thirteen days. On 8 August, she landed at Thiruvananthapuram airport at 2.30 p.m. Her visit was sponsored by Nasiha, daughter of her friend Fauziya Hassan. She flew to Bangalore with US $1700 for Fauziya the same day and stayed with her. The friends returned to Thiruvananthapuram on 17 September. Mariam's ninety-days period was to end one month later, i.e. 17 October 1994.

---

27. No: A-080493 issued by the Government of Maldives on 06.06.93 and valid till 05.06.98.
28. Circular No. 89 dated 1.3.90 issued by the Ministry of Home Affairs, Government of India, has exempted Maldivians from the requirement of Visa, provided their stay does not exceed 90 days during six months following their first entry to India in a calendar year.

On 8 October, she met Inspector Vijayan to obtain permission from the Commissioner for staying in India beyond 17 October. It is required under the seventh paragraph of the Foreigners Order, 1948. Mariam Rasheeda had legitimate grounds to stay beyond the deadline since Indian airlines had cancelled direct flights to the Maldives, indefinitely from 4 October 1994, following the plague scare in six Indian states.

Inspector Vijayan advised Mariam Rasheeda to get a confirmed ticket for her return. Accordingly, she purchased an Indian Airlines ticket – Thiruvananthapuram to Male (W/L), and another confirmed ticket of Sri Lankan Airlines – Thiruvananthapuram to Colombo, both for 17 October 1994. Vijayan took her travel documents and said that he needed them for processing her papers. She went to his office after three days, but he was not there.

On 12 October, the inspector went to Room 205, Hotel Samrat to get some clarifications from her. He asked Fauziya Hassan to wait outside.

"Mariam, you need not worry. You will get your papers ready, " he told her.

He then asked about her family. When she told him she was a divorcee, he moved closer to her and placed his hand on her shoulder, allowing his hand to slip down.

Fauziya was watching the busy road below when she heard Mariam's shrill voice. "Bas... you get out!"

She rushed back to her room and saw the inspector storming out of the room with sex still burning in his eyes and anger exploding from his cheeks, but his head down.

"I will finish you. I will complain to the IG. I know him personally," Mariam shouted at him, burning with fury.

The next day, she went to meet Vijayan at the Commissioner's office complex. And again, after two days. On both occasions, she couldn't meet him. Little did she know that he was at her hotel, searching for something that would help him pre-empt her move to file a complaint against him. At the same time, he wanted to take revenge for the humiliation she had inflicted on his male ego.

From the hotel sources, he learned that Mariam was a flirt. Telephone records showed she had been making calls to two numbers in Thiruvananthapuram and one in Mangalore. He left the Mangalore number and traced the holder of the first number in Thiruvananthapuram. It was D. Sasikumaran, Deputy Project Director, Cryogenic Project, Liquid Propellant Systems Centre who was residing near Ayurveda College, Thiruvananthapuram.

On 13 October, around 8.30 p.m., Inspector Vijayan tried that number.

"Sasikumar here."

"Do you know one Maldivian woman called Mariam Rasheeda?" Vijayan asked.

"Yes, she is staying in Hotel Samrat."

"Have you been to the hotel?"

"Yes."

"Have you ever taken her out?"

"Yes, but who are you to ask these questions?"

Vijayan didn't reply. He disconnected and tried the other number. To his surprise, it was the office number of the same Sasikumaran.

A flash went through his head.

Meanwhile, *Desabhimani*, a leading Malayalam daily, and *The Indian Communicator*, a low-profile English daily, had carried reports about foreigners who come to India without proper documents and later, jump bail. The stories hinted at a possible nexus between the airport authorities and some lawyers in the Thiruvananthapuram Bar abetting drug trafficking.

The City Police Commissioner V.R. Rajeevan IPS had issued an order on 15 October 1994 to the foreigners section to do random checking on the foreigners in Thiruvananthapuram. Finally, Inspector Vijayan got the opportunity he had been waiting for. He included Mariam Rasheeda in his random sample, suppressing the fact that her travel documents were with him. He could hide it since he had not recorded the seizure of her travel documents.

On 15 October, Inspector Vijayan questioned Mariam Rasheeda.

"What brought you here?"

"I brought money for my friend Fauziya's daughter's admission."

"What are you doing in the Maldives?"

"Working in the Army."

"Where is your identity card?"

She had none. She was a clerk in the personnel records section of the National Security Service from the latter part of 1988 to the first quarter of 1994. In her attempt to show off, she even told Vijayan that she was an agent of the Maldivian government to track down the anti-Maumoon Abdul Gayoom operations of some disgruntled Maldivians based in Bangalore.

Vijayan knitted the pieces together. As a policeman, he knew offence was the best form of defence. The same day, he met the Police Commissioner with a report that read thus:

> *On 15 October, while executing the orders of the Police Commissioner, I came across a Maldivian woman, Mariam Rasheeda who was overstaying in India since 14 October without any valid reason. I kept her under surveillance and found her in constant touch with an ISRO scientist.*

Vijayan presented ISRO as a centre linked to defence research, and the Police Commissioner swallowed it hook, line and sinker. On his part, the Commissioner informed the officials of IB and RAW about the possibility of a breakthrough in a major espionage case.

The IB sprang into action. So did RAW. The central outfits interrogated both Mariam Rasheeda and Fauziya Hassan first on 16 October and then on 19 October.

After the second round of interrogation was over, the Inspector tried to contact the correspondent of *Indian Communicator* who had filed the story about drug trafficking. When he couldn't find him, he contacted his journalist friend in *Thaniniram*, an eveninger, and leaked the news about a spy who had come to destroy India. He also gave an anonymous call to *Desabhimani*.

Once the story was set, Vijayan informed the Police Commissioner that the press had come to know of Mariam's detention. The Commissioner rang up R.B. Sreekumar, Deputy Director (IB), who told him that IB couldn't get anything incriminating from her. The Commissioner suggested that he could book her on grounds of overstay so that IB would get more time for further probe, and it was acceptable to Sreekumar. The Police Commissioner gave directions to Vijayan to arrest Mariam Rasheeda the next day.

It was on 20 October 1994.

Oblivious of the plot, Mariam telephoned Inspector Vijayan to find out whether her papers were ready. He asked her to come to his office at 4 p.m. By that time, the eveninger had flashed the news of her arrest. Only she didn't know it!

She waited in front of the office when the photographer of *Desabhimani* slowed his motorcycle in front of her and clicked a snap. Vijayan then called her in. He asked her to remove her ornaments and told her that she was under arrest. From there she was taken to Vanchiyoor Police Station where her arrest was officially made. She was then taken to the women's cell.

The next day, *Desabhimani* flashed its scoop.

Police have arrested a foreign defence officer on a mission to spy on India's PSLV technology. The Maldivian woman, Mariam Rasheeda, is a high-profile secret agent in the National Security Service. She had been in constant touch with a senior ISRO scientist and had contacted him thirteen times over the phone. The police have been closely monitoring the activities of foreigners following a report in this daily, a few days back, that foreign spies are having a free hand in the city.

Meanwhile, Inspector Vijayan prepared a report in Malayalam and got the draft corrected with the City Police Commissioner based on which the Commissioner sent a confidential letter[29] to the DGP. As per the confidential letter that became the genesis of the police version of Mariam Rasheeda's arrest, this is how Inspector Vijayan first met Mariam Rasheeda:

Since it was felt necessary to have some sort of watch over the movements of these Maldivian nationals, special instructions were given to the City Special Branch staff to form a special cell and verify hotel registers periodically. As part of such verification, on 15.10.94, the officers of the City Special Branch visited different hotels, lodging, etc., in Thiruvananthapuram City. S. Vijayan, Special Branch Inspector, noticed that a lady named Mariam Rasheeda, holder of Maldivian passport No. A- 080493, was residing in Room No 205 in Hotel Samrat at Thakaraparambu Road, East Fort, Thiruvananthapuram. Another Maldivian woman, Fauziya Hassan, holder of Maldivian Passport No. 057394 was also found staying in the same room...

29. No. SB/1053/G1/94-TC dated 24.10.1994

The Commissioner's letter is silent about Mariam Rasheeda's first visit to the inspector' office on 8 October 1994 since he was relying on a note submitted to his office by the inspector himself, who deliberately didn't mention anything about the meeting.

Inspector Vijayan gave another version of the whole episode in his report sent to Thampi S. Durgadatt, Sub-Inspector (SI), Vanchiyoor Police Station, requesting him to record Mariam Rasheeda's arrest. So, the arrest report, produced before the Additional CJM court on 21 October 1994 was in line with this new version. It reads:

> *Inspector Vijayan, through some sources, came to know that Mariam Rasheeda was in constant touch with scientists who are connected with the defence of India. On enquiry, he understood that she had shifted from Hotel Samrat to a rented house. On 20 October '94, he went to the house and verified her passport. He found her overstaying since 14 October. As she had violated Rule 7 of the Foreigners Order, 1948, and Section 14 of the Foreigners Act, 1946, she was detained in the interest of the sovereignty and integrity of the country, and later arrested.*

Vijayan presented ISRO as a defence organization to prevent any possible counter-allegation from Mariam Rasheeda regarding his misbehaviour. He was sure any such allegation would become a damp squib if Mariam Rasheeda was presented as a spy who had come to destabilize the sovereignty and integrity of India.

Now, which among the two records tells a lie?

Both, if you go by the judgment of the Chief Judicial Magistrate, Ernakulam[30]. The judgment delivered a year and 24 days after her arrest reads:

---

30. C.C. No. 1464/94, the Overstay Case of Mariam Rasheeda

It is apparent that 17 October 1994 was the last day permissible for the stay of the accused in India.

This finding demolishes the very basis of the Commissioner's theory. This clarifies that Inspector Vijayan had no reason to suspect Mariam Rasheeda when he checked her passport on 15 October.

The police version that Mariam Rasheeda was overstaying since 14 October and that she couldn't give valid reasons for her overstay when Inspector Vijayan checked her passport the next day, therefore, is a lie.

It was clear. Not overstaying, but something else motivated Vijayan to keep surveillance over Mariam. The judgment gives a clue.

In fact, she was chased by the police party consisting of Inspector Vijayan and others at least from the middle of October, obstructing her from leaving India.

The word 'obstruction' has special significance. It means Inspector Vijayan had seized her travel documents – a fact both Inspector Vijayan and the Commissioner suppressed.

The judge asserts:

"I find no reason to disbelieve the defence version that the air tickets were recovered by Inspector Vijayan from Mariam Rasheeda with the intention of obstructing her from leaving India for the purpose of arresting her on grounds of overstay."

But, Inspector Vijayan denied having seized Mariam Rasheeda's travel documents

Why should Inspector Vijayan suppress certain vital information before the court of law when he had every right to seize her travel documents if she was overstaying when he checked her passport?

The judgment disproves Inspector Vijayan's statement in his report to the Sub-Inspector of Vanchiyoor Police Station that he encountered Mariam Rasheeda only on 20 October – the date of her arrest.

The judgment reads: *Inspector Vijayan has further deposed in cross-examination that before the accused was arrested, he had the opportunity to see and question her on two occasions. He had questioned her at Hotel Samrat two or three days before her arrest and also at the office of the City Police Commissioner.*

Inspector Vijayan went to Hotel Samrat and met Mariam Rasheeda in her room. He didn't want to put on record that he had touched her body and that she had humiliated him. The judgment throws light on Inspector Vijayan's dubious nature. He evaded from disclosing his first meeting with Mariam Rasheeda by saying that he did not remember.

It is strange that a police officer who claimed to have cracked a spy ring 'working to destabilise the sovereignty of the nation' couldn't remember the date on which he met the queen bee of the ring. He couldn't afford to remember, as it would reveal many unpleasant things.

However, Mariam Rasheeda took a consistent stand that she was a victim of Inspector Vijayan's sexual frustration. She said it first to the *Savvy* magazine (April 1996) in an interview she gave me. Though Vijayan filed a defamation case against the magazine and Mariam Rasheeda for saying it (the court dismissed the case), Mariam repeated the allegation in her petition to the NHRC (19 July 1996) and the Kerala Women's Commission (23 July 1997), besides her letter to the Chief Justice of India (1 February 1997). The Supreme Court accepted her letter as a Special Leave Petition and engaged a lawyer for her.

Though Inspector Vijayan repeatedly claimed that he had suspected her to be a spy, the CJM's judgment provides ample ammunition to blast his theory.

It was noted that all movables of the accused, excluding her wearing apparels and the citizen watch, were with Mohammed Nayim (Mariam's relative) even on the date of her arrest. Nayim was allowed to return to Maldives with Mariam Rasheeda's things, after she was arrested. Will any police officer, who keeps track of a spy, ever allow a relative of the prime accused to leave India with her movables after her arrest?

The dubious moves of Inspector Vijayan, with the connivance of Police Commissioner V.R. Rajeevan, even after the arrest of Mariam Rasheeda, need a lot of explaining.

▼

Some more questions become relevant at this stage.

- The Additional Chief Judicial Magistrate, Thiruvananthapuram, remanded Mariam Rasheeda to police custody, specifically under the custody of Inspector Vijayan, on 3 November 1994. But he entrusted her to the IB officials for interrogation – a flagrant case of dereliction of duty with regard to the court order.

Was the Police Commissioner unaware of this illegal act?

- Inspector Vijayan brought photographs of Raman Srivastava, both in uniform and mufti, and forced Mariam Rasheeda to identify them. Raman Srivastava, IG (South Zone) was the immediate boss of V. R. Rajeevan, the Police Commissioner.

Did Vijayan do it without the knowledge of the Commissioner?

- The remand report of Mariam Rasheeda, dated 14 November 1994, submitted before the CJM seeking extension of her custody bears the signature of Inspector Vijayan. The court extended the custody and returned her to Inspector Vijayan. The Government of Kerala constituted an SIT the next day, and Vijayan handed her over to the SIT. It is what the police records say.

But another official record tells a different story.

- The inpatient register of the Government Hospital for Contagious Diseases, Airanimuttom, Thiruvananthapuram, shows that Inspector Vijayan was admitted to the hospital on 14 November 1994 at 10.50 a.m. since he had contracted chickenpox and that he was discharged after ten days. The column bears his signature.

Now, how could Inspector Vijayan, admitted as a chickenpox patient in a hospital at 10.50 a.m., report before the court which commences only at 11 a.m.?

Does it mean the chickenpox patient produced the accused before the court himself?

If so, what prevented him from submitting before the court, orally or in writing that the accused be given under the custody of some other police officer since he was an inpatient suffering from chickenpox?

Where did Inspector Vijayan keep Mariam Rasheeda from the time she was remanded under his custody (14 November 94, 11 a.m.) till he handed her over to Siby Mathews DIG, the leader of SIT, the next day?

How could the Police Commissioner be oblivious of all these? Interestingly, when the SIT was constituted the next day, Inspector Vijayan was a member of it. What makes Inspector Vijayan an unavoidable character in the whole drama, even after he had contracted chickenpox?

Before we ponder over these uncomfortable questions, it is time to expose the second layer of the plot hatched a day after Mariam Rasheeda's arrest.

5

The Wrath of an Editor

22 October 1994; 10.30 a.m.

It was a warm Tuesday, two days after the arrest of Mariam Rasheeda. Raman Srivastava, IG (South Zone), P.R. Chandran, IG (Computer Wing) and a couple of DIGs were sitting in Aravind Ranjan's office, DIG, Administration, in the Police Headquarters, Thiruvananthapuram. They were there to meet T.V. Madhusoodanan, DGP, for the final round of talks regarding the recommendation of officers for the President's Medal.

Intelligence DIG then told Raman Srivastava about a front-page report in *Kerala Kaumudi*, a Malayalam newspaper, linking his name to Mariam Rasheeda and the spy ring. He read out the story to the IG and advised him to sue the paper.

"Newspapers carry all sorts of stories. If we start denying every news item, there won't be any end to it," Srivastava replied.

Srivastava recollected what the Commissioner had told him two days ago, over the phone. "A lady from the Maldives by the name Mariam Rasheeda has been apprehended since the 15th. Officers from the IB, RAW and the Special Branch have questioned her. There are some suspicions. But there is no evidence to book her under anything except for overstay."

Raman Srivastava, the Commissioner's immediate boss, gave his nod to proceed on the lines suggested by the Commissioner after obtaining the concurrence of the DGP. *Why such a news item linking my name to some spy ring?* Srivastava wondered.

It was then that P.R. Chandran said that he knew Mariam Rasheeda. "She had met me once or twice regarding some visa problem of her friend's daughter studying in Bangalore. Mariam was introduced to me by Sasikumaran, a scientist in ISRO. He is a friend."

Maybe, Srivastava thought, the newspaper had mistaken P.R. Chandran for him and misinterpreted the humane gesture as hobnobbing with a spy.

The meeting with the DGP lasted for less than thirty minutes. The DGP didn't ask Srivastava anything about the newspaper report. But Srivastava told his boss that in the light of the newspaper report, he was keeping away from the investigation, which he otherwise should have supervised. The DGP agreed. The decision was communicated to the commissioner also. Meanwhile, P.R. Chandran informed the DGP that Mariam Rasheeda had met him once or twice when he had sorted out the visa problem of Fauziya Hassan's daughter through his batch-mate, Mr Bhaskar, at Bangalore. The matter ended there.

The next day, *Kerala Kaumudi* whipped Srivastava. Its kicker headline yelled, *DGP Sought Explanation from Srivastava.*

> *The DGP summoned Raman Srivastava IG (south zone) to his office and sought an explanation about his links with the spy from Maldives. The meeting lasted for an hour. The DGP questioned him about the dates on which he had met Mariam Rasheeda and the circumstances under which he developed links with the spy. The DGP is reported to be unhappy with the explanations of Srivastava. He is also understood to have asked the IG to come out with a satisfactory explanation about the whole affair.*

For a few days to follow, Raman Srivastava was on *Kerala Kaumudi's* target. The newspaper carried fabricated stories one after the other – he had close links with more than one spy ring; the personal computer of ISRO scientist Sasikumaran had details about the IG's spying activities; he had slept with Mariam Rasheeda in Bombay and Madras; he used his forged passport for his foreign trips; he was known as 'Brigadier' or '*Coatwallah*' in the spy ring; he had purchased three thousand acres of land in Tirunelveli in Tamil Nadu and runs prawn farms there; he had *benami* business dealings at Tanjore; his business in Tanjore had links with both ISI and LTTE, and so on.

The highly explosive reports forced other newspapers, including some South Indian language newspapers and national newspapers, to come out with their own 'scoops' on Raman Srivastava, for the fear of being pushed back in the rat race. From New Delhi, *Hindustan Times* chipped in with a report that the IG had share certificates to the tune of Rs 7.5 crore. The sensation created was so powerful that Raman Srivastava emerged as the kingpin of the spy ring.

But, why did *Kerala Kaumudi* frame Raman Srivastava?

Not many know Raman Srivastava was the *bete noire* of M.S. Mani, the then Editor of *Kerala Kaumudi*. It is a long story at the end of which you see Raman Srivastava and M.S. Mani locking horns.

Kerala Kaumudi was founded in 1911 as a weekly to air the voice of the backward Ezhava community. Eventually, it became a newspaper in 1940 with K. Sukumaran as its sole proprietor. Fifteen years later, K. Sukumaran and his wife C.N. Madhavi promoted *Kerala Kaumudi* as a private limited company. K. Sukumaran was the Managing Director till 1973 and remained the Chairman till his death in 1981. Meanwhile, the nation honoured him with Padma Bhushan.

M.S. Mani, eldest of his four sons, joined the editorial wing even before he became a graduate and soon rose to become the youngest editor of a newspaper in India. His brother, M.S. Madhusoodanan, became the Managing Director in 1973, a year which proved to be a watershed in the history of the paper.

On 13 September 1973, *Kerala Kaumudi* carried an investigative report on the illegal felling of trees in Kerala. The story rocked the state government and put the Forest Minister K.G. Adiyodi, a protégé of Congress leader K. Karunakaran who was then the Home Minister of Kerala, in the dock. The government retaliated by ordering an inquiry by High Court Judge V. Balakrishna Eradi.

The backfire cost M.S. Mani his editorship and he started *Kala Kaumudi* weekly on 17 July 1975. Madhusoodanan assumed the dual role of the Editor and Managing Director of Kerala Kaumudi. On 23 April 1985, M.S. Mani resigned from the Board of Directors, airing his protest over the policy of the paper because under Madhusoodanan, the pro-Left paper had become pro-Congress.

Meanwhile, Madhavi Sukumaran, the Chairperson, circulated a thirty-three-page note to the shareholders, raising serious allegations against M.S. Madhusoodanan. The son, in turn, made a counter-attack, alleging his mother and brother M. S. Sreenivasan were selling newsprint in the black market with the connivance of their bank, disregarding his repeated warnings.

A series of dramatic events followed.

- Madhavi Sukumaran and her two younger sons, M.S. Sreenivasan and M.S. Ravi, filed a suit against M.S. Mani and M.S. Madhusoodanan for partition of the nine shares owned by the late K. Sukumaran.
- Madhusoodanan's wife Geetha arrived at her office on 4 August 1986 in the Kaumudi Buildings, but was denied the key. She moved to court seeking an injunction to restrain her mother-in-law and M.S. Mani from disturbing her office functions.

- The General Body removed M.S. Madhusoodanan from the Board of Directors. Madhusoodanan, in turn, moved to High Court on 27 September 1986.
- A Single Bench of Kerala High Court reinstated M.S. Madhusoodanan as Editor and Managing Director on 15 March 1990.
- M.S. Mani didn't vacate the office, so Madhusoodanan moved a contempt of court petition before the High Court. The court directed the Commissioner of Police, Thiruvananthapuram, to implement the court order.
- M.S. Mani went to the office of Raman Srivastava, the Commissioner of Police, and pleaded with him to delay the implementation of the court order at least by a week so that he could try for a stay from the Division Bench. Raman Srivastava told him bluntly that "the court orders have to be enforced".
- Armed with the order from the High Court, M.S. Madhusoodanan, escorted by a contingent of the police force under Raman Srivastava, entered the office premises on 22 March 1990.
- The police gate crashed into the premises as the entrance was locked from inside. Raman Srivastava ordered his force to clear a gang of paid goons positioned in the premises. The police physically pulled M.S. Mani, the Editor, out of his chair when he refused to vacate the seat. M.S. Madhusoodanan occupied the chair of the Editor and threw M.S. Mani's name board into the dust bin.
- M.S. Mani stood silent with his head down. But the worst was still to come. He was pushed out of the premises. He stood near a transformer in front of the building for a while when a group collected around him. He then walked towards Pettah

Police Station, near his old office, where he organized a public meeting.

- A wounded M.S. Mani declared that he would destroy Raman Srivastava.

Many things happened since that incident. A Division Bench quashed the order of the Single Bench and Madhusoodanan moved to the Supreme Court. M.S. Mani became Editor of *Kerala Kaumudi* once again.

Four years and seven months later, *Kerala Kaumudi* implicated Raman Srivastava, now an IG, in the spy scandal by filing a false and baseless story that Raman Srivastava was a member of the spy ring. M.S. Mani kept the tempo going because of a couple of trusted journalists. Records with the police and the jail authorities show that *Kerala Kaumudi* had implicated Raman Srivastava without any evidence.

Mariam Rasheeda was arrested at 4.15 p.m. on 20 October 1994. She was produced before the Magistrate the next morning. Vanchiyoor Police Station or the women's cell has no records to establish that she was questioned. Whereas, the Police Commissioner's letter to the DGP dated 24 October 1994 makes it clear that Mariam Rasheeda was questioned by IB, RAW and Kerala Police on two occasions before her arrest. The letter, written on 24 October 1994, two days after *Kerala Kaumudi* had implicated Srivastava in the case, has no mention of Raman Srivastava.

Case diaries of the Kerala Police, reports of IB, and the Closure Report of CBI tell in one voice that Mariam Rasheeda "didn't say anything incriminating during the first week of her interrogation."

Her interrogation began on 3 November 1994 because she was under judicial custody from 21 October to 3 November. The most incriminating fact in the forced 'confession' of Mariam Rasheeda is her identification of Raman Srivastava as a member of the spy ring.

The case diaries reveal that Mariam Rasheeda named Raman Srivastava after 8 November. When CBI concluded that she was tortured to name Srivastava (which is what she told me in her interview for *Savvy* magazine), IB and Kerala Police held that she named him on her own. On 9 November, Inspector Vijayan had met Raman Srivastava at his house and informed the IG that Mariam Rasheeda had named him.

All these facts point to one conclusion – Mariam Rasheeda named Raman Srivastava, only after she was remanded to police custody on 3 November 1994.

Then, from where did *Kerala Kaumudi* get the explosive information about Raman Srivastava's involvement in the spy ring as early as 21 October 1994?

Did any of its journalists meet her either at Vanchiyoor Police Station or the women cell on the night of 20 October to get the explosive disclosure that IB or RAW couldn't bring out from her? The records say – No.

Did any of its journalists meet her in the jail on 21 October? The jail records say – No.

If so, how did the name of Raman Srivastava appear out of the blue?

Its answer takes us to a story of revenge.

▼

When Mariam Rasheeda was produced before the Magistrate at Thiruvananthapuram on 21 October, she engaged a lawyer who she thought was a Muslim because of his thin beard with neatly trimmed sides and prayer bump-like marking on the forehead. She told him she knew the IG and had met him twice. She had P.R. Chandran in her mind who she had met, as suggested by D. Sasikumaran, in connection with the visa problem of Fauziya Hassan's daughter. But the advocate interpreted it as Raman Srivastava since he had an axe to grind against Raman Srivastava, who had once humiliated him and had asked him to get out of his office when he had argued with the IG regarding the implementation of helmets for bike riders.

The advocate made phone calls to all newspaper offices and informed them about Mariam Rasheeda's closeness with Raman Srivastava. While most of the reporters ignored the information partly because of Srivastava's close connections with the all-powerful Chief Minister K. Karunakaran and partly because of the low credibility of the advocate, *Kerala Kaumudi* gave it a deadly twist because of its Editor M.S. Mani's enmity towards Raman Srivastava. Apart from fixing Raman Srivastava, M.S Mani thought it was the right time to settle scores with K. Karunakaran, the then Chief Minister of Kerala.

By implicating Raman Srivastava in the spy ring, *Kerala Kaumudi* aimed to paint K. Karunakaran as a traitor, since Srivastava, described as the shadow of K. Karunakaran, was his blue-eyed boy.

Two birds in one shot.

Even as a police inspector and an editor were taking vengeance on those who had wounded their egos, someone else at a faraway place was watching the drama with great curiosity. That someone was the CIA. And there were many reasons for that.

6

Force Majeure

800-1/50 was a bilateral agreement signed between Glavkosmos, the Russian space agency, and ISRO on 18 January 1991 (when Russia was a part of the Soviet Union). It envisaged supply of three cryogenic stages, KVD-1, built by the Isayev Design Bureau, and the transfer of cryogenic rocket technology to ISRO for Rs 235 crore.

The US openly expressed its displeasure over the transfer of technology and began to arm-twist Russia using political pressure and economic sanctions to cancel the agreement. On 20 July 1993, Russia cancelled the ISRO-Glavkosmos agreement, invoking *force majeure*.

Force majeure is a contract provision that relieves the parties from performing their contractual obligations when certain circumstances beyond their control arise, making performance inadvisable, commercially impracticable, illegal or impossible.

Provisions often cover natural disasters like hurricanes, floods, earthquakes and weather disturbances, sometimes referred to as 'acts of god'. Other covered events include war, terrorism or threats of terrorism, civil disorder, labour strikes or disruptions, fire, disease or medical epidemics or outbreaks.

For Russia, *force majeure* was the political earthquake in the Soviet Union that dismembered the USSR, with Russia becoming an independent country on 26 December 1991.

A modified agreement, without the crucial technology transfer clause, was signed between ISRO and Glavkosmos in January 1994. With that, Russia fully protected the US commercial interest.

Facts being so, why did the CIA plant the espionage case in November 1994, sixteen months after America had succeeded in stopping the transfer of Russian cryogenic technology to India?

▼

The transfer of cryogenic rocket technology was aimed to take India to the space club as a nation capable of launching satellites into the geosynchronous orbit (GSO), close to 35, 768 kilometres away from the earth. It was the third major step in the Indian rocketry programme since India bought the solid propellant technology from Sud-Aviation in 1967 and liquid technology, ten years later, from Ariane, both in France. India started negotiating with US and France for buying cryogenic technology.

It was in the middle of the 1980s. While the American company General Dynamics quoted Rs 950 crore for the engines and technology transfer, the French company Aerospatiale quoted Rs 650 crore. India was in two minds – whether to opt for the US deal, thus heralding a new trade friendship with the United States, or to buy from France, the tested trade friend, for a lower price.

But before the final round of negotiations were to begin, Glavkosmos, the Russian space agency entered the market with a throw away price of Rs 235 crore for a package of cryogenic stages and technology, causing great embarrassment to both America and France.

This time, India had no hesitation. Glavkosmos was not undercutting. Being a novice in international trade, it was not fully aware of the big margin of profit in the space market. Also, Glavkosmos, like any other organization in Russia, was badly in need of money following the collapse of the Soviet Union and the introduction of Yeltsin's new economic policy.

After signing the historic treaty with Russia, India was all poised to have its counter opened, with the Department of Space drafting the master plan to transform ISRO into a commercial outfit taking orders from other countries to launch their satellites at GSO. The success of PSLV which injects a satellite at 817 km above the earth is peanuts compared to the technological supremacy of GSLV that could launch satellites into the GSO at a height of 35, 786 km.

But the agreement went against the US commercial interest in two ways. Firstly, the price quoted by Glavkosmos was nearly 400% less than what America's General Dynamics had quoted. The undercut caused serious concern over the future sales of American rocket technology, elsewhere. Secondly, the proposed price-per-kg-payload for GSLV to inject satellites into the GSO was less than half the price quoted by the US vehicles.

The high-profit space market is controlled essentially by five countries – America, France, Russia, China and Japan. They are capable of sending satellites to the GSO using the cryogenic engine. USA has three commercial vehicles that take satellites to the GSO – Titan IV, Delta, and Atlas. France has one, Ariane-4. Russia, China, and Japan have one each – Proton, Long March3, and H2, respectively.

A typical cost-per-kg of payload offered by the vehicles is – For Titan IV, it is $43, 000; Delta, $31, 000; Atlas, $35, 000, Ariane -4, $28, 000; Proton, $22, 000; H2, $33, 000; and LongMarch 3, $20, 000. The proposed cost-per-kg of payload offered by India's GSLV was below $18, 000.

The difference is overt. With its payload price tentatively fixed at less than half the price charged by the US launch vehicles, ISRO anticipated nearly 50% of the 300 billion dollar space market by 2010. The potential damage to the US commercial interest is better understood when one understands that a large chunk of the space market was and is being appropriated by the US space players.

▼

Within a few months after the ISRO-Glavkosmos agreement was inked, the then US State Secretary sent a letter to his Soviet counterpart expressing America's displeasure over the agreement. The US opposed the sale of cryogenic engine technology on the grounds that it violated the 1987 MTCR. But the agreement, when it was signed, did not violate the MTCR since the rule of MTCR, as on the date of signing the contract, had exempted orbit correction engines from the list of banned technologies.

Moreover, cryogenic engines meant for space rockets have little utility for ballistic missiles as the fuelling of such space rockets takes several days. Such a procedure would have little relevance for military use since missiles are intended to be deployable at short notice.

Yet, on 11 May 1992, the US imposed sanctions on ISRO and Glavkosmos.

A report of the Federation of American Scientists (FAS), an American non-profit global policy think tank, reads:

> *(Text: Boucher statement on sanctions) (480) Washington – The United States has imposed sanctions against the Russian space organization Glavkosmos and the Indian Space Research Organization (ISRO) because of the transfer of rocket engine technology, says State Department Deputy Spokesman Richard Boucher.*
>
> *The transfer, he said in a statement issued May 11, "is inconsistent with" Missile Technology Control Regime (MTCR) guidelines. Boucher said the sanctions against the two entities include a two-year ban on all U.S. licensed exports, on all imports into the United States, and on U.S. government contracts.*

"Our principal objective...is to obtain the broadest possible international cooperation in curbing the dangerous proliferation of missile technology," the deputy spokesman said.

Following is the text of Boucher's statement: For some time the United States and other member countries of the Missile Technology Control Regime (MTCR) have been involved in discussions – first with the former Soviet government and now with the Russian government – about the serious concerns we have with the transfer of rocket engine technology from Glavkosmos to the Indian Space Research Organization (ISRO). We have also been discussing our concerns directly with the Indian government.

The MTCR guidelines provide the international standard for such matters. The MTCR partners have concluded that the Glavkosmos-ISRO deal is inconsistent with the MTCR guidelines. That is why they have urged that this deal not go through.

For its part, the United States in its discussions with Russia and India has also made clear that U.S. law requires sanctions against entities engaged in activities inconsistent with MTCR guidelines. Since the facts are clear and since the parties to the transaction have declined to terminate these activities, the United States has imposed sanctions in accordance with our law. The sanctions are:

- *A two-year ban on all U.S. licensed exports to these entities (i.e., Glavkosmos and ISRO);*
- *A two-year ban on all imports into the United States from these entities; and*
- *A two-year ban on U.S. government contracts with these entities. We are continuing to pursue discussion of this issue with both governments. We have explained to both*

> *governments that termination of the Glavkosmos-ISRO deal could permit us to consider a waiver of these sanctions.*[31]
>
> *The sanction was followed by more bullying on Russia, a new country, by the US. The US Senate Foreign Relations Committee added conditions to an aid deal, proposed by then US President George H.W. Bush that would transfer $24 billion to Russia. An amendment that banned US aid to any former Soviet republic that transferred missile, nuclear, or chemical weapons technology abroad was moved by the Committee Member Joe Biden, then the Senator from Delaware. "I am confident that the Russian leaders will recognize the wisdom of stopping this sale (transfer of cryogenic technology from Glavkosmos to ISRO) once they see the risk of losing their economic aid... This is no minor sale; this is dangerous, " Biden said. (Los Angeles Times, 14 May 1992).*

It was a two-pronged trade war – to stop Russia from hard-selling high-tech know-how, and to prevent India from emerging as a new member of the GSO oligopoly. Russia didn't protest. They couldn't. Being one of the signatories of MTCR, they were bound to abide by any amendments to it.

Also, the US had already forced Russia to sign a pact with other members of the space club that Russia would not quote less than 90% of what any other member would quote in the international market.

The US could arm-twist Russia because the history of the world had undergone a sea-change by that time. As the world map had to be redrawn, boundaries crossed or vanished.

By December 1991, the mighty Soviet Union was reduced to an ash heap. Mikhail Gorbachev breathed in more oxygen into the

31. *https://fas.org/nuke/control/mtcr/news/920511-227224.htm*

tailor-made psyche of the comrades, while George Bush set fire to it through his Man Friday, Boris Yeltsin. All this was done after the Swedish Academy had crucified the Glasnost messiah on a Nobel Prize for Peace, from where neither he nor his country resurrected. The bipolar power equation became unipolar with the American Presidency transforming the world into a police state.

Russia lost Russia in Russia.

India didn't protest. India could have. India was not a signatory to the MTCR when the agreement was signed.[32] But nobody in India made a hue and cry – politicians, technocrats or media. No lobbying was done to reverse the lie that India's acquiring cryogenic technology was linked to its missile programme.

The scientific community that knew the truth preferred to be silent. The politicians, oblivious of the world around them, were confined to their fiefdom. The media, which ought to have brought the truth to the people, were happy airing lies that came in handy.

An international treaty was scrapped like a soiled sheet of paper.In April 1993, Russian President Boris Yeltsin reached a 'compromise' with the new US president Bill Clinton on the cryogenic engine deal with India at a meeting in Vancouver. On 20 July 1993, Russia cancelled the agreement, invoking *force majeure*. A modified agreement was signed between ISRO and Glavkosmos in January 1994. The agreement didn't have the technology transfer clause.

While the Clinton administration was happy that its commercial interests were well protected by Yeltsin, there were voices of dissent in Russia. The Russian Parliament (Duma) was in no mood to let President Boris Yeltsin bail on India. On 20 July 1993, the Duma passed a resolution declaring that international negotiations and

---

32 India joined as the 35thmember of MTCR on 27 June 2016.

agreements regarding the MTCR must be ratified by the Supreme Soviet of the Russian Federation.

A report by Daniel Sneider that appeared in The *Christian Science Monitor* on 27 July 1993, bearing the headline 'Russians Up in Arms about Cancellation of Rocket Deal' would tell it in detail.

> *After months of tough negotiations with the United States, a Russian government delegation announced in Washington last week their decision to join international controls on missile technology and to halt an ongoing transfer of missile know-how to India.*
>
> *The deal was hailed in Washington as yet another sign of Russia's growing partnership with the West. But back home it is being assailed as one more case of Russia yielding its national interests to American domination.*
>
> *"If the contract is scrapped, it will be a national disgrace for Russia," Parliament Chairman Ruslan Khasbulatov, a rival of President Boris Yeltsin, told deputies on 21 July 1993.*
>
> *"This issue...has become a criterion for the independence of Russian foreign policy," declared a July 16 statement of Civic Union, a bloc of opposition parties. "The interests of the country are exchanged by those in power for the political support of the USA, " the group charged.*
>
> *The controversy over the contract to supply India with cryogenic rocket boosters has been raging since last year. The US claims the deal, particularly the supply of the technological information to produce such rocket engines, would enable India to launch not only commercial space vehicles, such as satellites but military missiles. Both Russian and Indian officials have argued that the technology can be used only for peaceful purposes.*
>
> *Until recently, the Russian government resisted US pressure to back out of the contract. But the US raised the ante, tying Russian*

compliance with the MTCR with promises to give the Russian space programme access to the commercial satellite market and participation in the US programme to build a space station. A planned June visit of Russian Premier Viktor Chernomyrdin was postponed at the last minute when negotiators failed to reach an agreement on the India issue.

The Russian government's decision was announced by Yuri Koptev, head of the Russian Space Agency, on July 20 in Washington after a week of talks. Mr Koptev said Russia would sign the MTCR and as a consequence revise its contract with India. Russia is prepared to supply India with ready-made engines but will not transfer any further technology or production facilities.

The main Russian partner in the India deal, Glavkosmos, the commercial arm of the Russian space industry has objected to the announcement. Glavkosmos officials argue that Koptev did not have the authority to make such a decision, that the Foreign Ministry also did not have the right to alter the Indian contract and they back the assertion that the Russian parliament must ratify the MTCR.

Anatoly Tkachyov, a spokesman for the Russian Space Agency, concurred with the Glavkosmos assertion that the Russian delegation in Washington did not have the authority to make a final decision. "The agreement in Washington was not signed but only initialled," he said. "It must still be signed by Premier Chernomyrdin, who will visit Washington in August, and ratified by the parliament.

"The agreement was signed by authorized representatives of the Russian government," commented a senior US diplomat, speaking to reporters on July 22. "The question of ratification is an internal one. As with all agreements carried out in good faith between governments...we would expect the Russian government will do whatever is necessary to carry out that agreement."

7

Reverse Espionage

22 July 1993

The difference of opinion on scrapping the agreement was very much evident in Glavkosmos when Glavkosmos spokesman Nikolai Semyonov came out in the open and said, "We shall not stop fulfilling our obligations under the contract until there is a governmental decision to the contrary, " upping its pressure on Yeltsin.

Aleksey V. Vasin, the officer in charge of the cryogenic system in Glavkosmos, took a strong stand that cryogenic rocket technology should be transferred to ISRO, for which he had the wholehearted support of Chairman Alexander I. Dunayev. The pro-Indian camp in Glavkosmos got an equally enthusiastic reciprocation from Prof. U.R. Rao, Chairman of ISRO. Both parties knew they were planning to execute it clandestinely, hoodwinking the US.

While Aleksey Vasin was the go-getter in Glavkosmos, his counterpart in ISRO was S. Nambi Narayanan. They worked out two plans with the full knowledge of the top brass in both Glavkosmos and ISRO.

Their first plan was to illegally transport raw materials, pieces of equipment, drawings, spare parts and other sensitive materials that were part of technology transfer under the scrapped contract, from Glavkosmos to ISRO, using stealthy modes.

It sounded good for both parties. However, Glavkosmos was not ready for door delivery since the operation had to be done keeping the Russian government in the dark and hoodwinking the US intelligence network. The job had to be done by ISRO, while Glavkosmos would provide all necessary help and facilitate the transfer, which both parties knew would be violating the amended MTCR.

The second plan was to transfer the cryogenic technology to an Indian company as an off-shore partner to fabricate the cryogenic engines meant for India. ISRO could later get the technology transferred from that company – an unofficial process which Glavkosmos would pretend not to be aware of.

An Illegal Trajectory

A furtive strategy was designed to transfer drawings, instruments, spare parts and equipments of cryogenic rocket technology, directly to ISRO.

Since Glavkosmos was not ready for door delivery and wanted ISRO to take the risk, Nambi Narayanan contacted Air India. But Air India insisted on proper documents which ISRO didn't have; a clear indication that the transportation was far from legal. Nambi Narayanan then struck a deal with Url Aviation, a Russian airliner, by offering extra money to transport materials from Glavkosmos to ISRO without proper and legally valid documents, clandestinely, using different air routes to avoid suspicion of the strong US lobby in Glavkosmos and Russia.

As D. Sasikumaran, Deputy Director (Fabrication) of the Cryogenic Technology Division of ISRO and in-charge of the cryogenic technology transfer from Glavkosmos, later told *Kaumudi* Television Channel, the "situation was so critical that we had to take things to the airport in the jeep, secretly, to escape the American eyes and that of a section in Glavkosmos itself."

Though there were five airports in Moscow, where Glavkosmos has its headquarters, the situation was so critical that it was not possible to airlift anything from any of the five airports, tricking the US surveillance. The go-getters in Glavkosmos and ISRO then decided to hoodwink the US by first transporting the cargo to some other destination by road and then to airlift it from there to India using different Url flights that took different air routes.

The destination they zeroed in on was the international airport at Tashkent in Uzbekistan, one of the fifteen republics of the former USSR that had become an independent republic on 1 September 1991, three months before the formal collapse of the Soviet Union.

Once the logistics were finalized, the materials were stealthily transported from Glavkosmos to Tashkent through road in trucks, covering 3,376 km, from where they were airlifted to Thiruvananthapuram in Url flights coming from Moscow.

The first flight of Url 224 from Russia took the Karachi route and landed at Thiruvananthapuram on 23 January 1994; the second flight, Url 9001, landed on 11 March 1994; and the third, Url 3791, took Russia-Sharjah route and landed at Thiruvananthapuram on 17 July 1994. As a cover, Indian aircraft technology for testing in Russian wind-tunnels was transported in the return flights of Url Aviation. S. Nambi Narayanan was on board the first flight of Url Aviation.

More flights were to come. The fourth Url flight was scheduled to reach Thiruvananthapuram by the middle of November. It didn't come. The spy scandal stopped it.

A Clandestine Trajectory

The idea was to transfer the cryogenic rocket technology to India through a clandestine operation, fooling the US surveillance. As part of it, a strategy was designed to entrust the work of fabricating cryogenic engines to an external agency as job work, though no off-shore partner was part of first or second agreement between ISRO and Glavkosmos.

The agency both parties zeroed in on was Kerala Hi-tech Industries Limited (KELTEC) in Thiruvananthapuram, the present BrahMos Aerospace, specialising in hi-tech fabrication works. To fabricate cryogenic engine, its technology needed to be transferred to KELTC. This transfer, both parties knew, would not attract the provisions of MTCR. The clandestine move was meticulously planned.

The technology transfer aspect is evident in a note sent by V. Sudhakar, Managing Director, KELTEC, to Alexander I. Dunayev, Chairman, Glavkosmos, on 8 January 1993, six months before Russia unilaterally cancelled the first ISRO-Glavkosmos agreement invoking *force majeure*. The note reads, "KELTEC is now negotiating with ISRO for the fabrication and supply of Cryo Engines for which technology is supplied by Russia."

A few correspondences between Glavkosmos and KELTEC that began on 4 March 1992 tell volumes about the clandestine operation that was in the offing, but finally got aborted in the wake of the espionage case.

- On 4 March 1992, Aleksey V. Vasin had an official meeting with V. Sudhakar, Managing Director of KELTEC, at the latter's office. Minutes of the meeting signed by both the parties read:

  Mr Aleksey indicated that KELTEC's facility can be utilized in realization of systems connected with Cryo project for which they have signed an agreement with ISRO. Mr Aleksey disclosed that his team of experts will make a visit to KELTEC in May 1992 for further development of a business relationship with KELTEC.

- A telex message from V. Sudhakar to ISRO Chairman U.R. Rao[33] and K. Chandrasekhar, Representative, Glavkosmos reads:

  Mr Aleksey's visit to KELTEC was followed by the visit of M/S M. Siracheve (Chief Designer) and V. Mitansov (Chief of Production) on 6 March. They expressed their satisfaction of the facilities available/ planned at KELTEC for the manufacture of Cryo system for GSLV. According to them, more than 95 percent of the facilities are available at KELTEC. They were also highly impressed with our types of equipment and setup. This is for your information, please."

- On 8 January 1993, V. Sudhakar sent a letter[34] to Alexander I. Dunayev[35], inviting his team to KELTEC. He had enclosed a Note to Dunayev as a proposal for a joint venture between Glavkosmos and KELTEC with equity participation and mobilization of balance financing necessary through public issues, and a 10-page annexure showing its financial projection, working results, and profitability projection. The joint venture contemplated was a Rs 1,000-million project. Finance was to be raised through Government of Kerala-Equity Rs 130 million, minimum suggested Glavkosmos Equity 130, and present loans, 250. Balance Rs 490 million was to be raised from capital markets. (It is in this note that Sudhakar states, *"KELTEC is now negotiating with ISRO for the fabrication and supply of Cryo Engines for which technology is supplied by Russia."*)
- A high-power delegation led by Glavkosmos Chairman A. I. Dunayev agreed to invest money in the joint venture from

---

33. Ref. No. KELTEC/A6/817, dated 9 March 1992, faxed at 13. 28 IST, with a copy marked to Dr A.E. Muthunayagam, Director, LPSC; Dr S.C. Gupta, Director, VSSC; R. Jayamani, Project Director, GSLV, VSSC
34. D.O. No.KELTEC/B6-5/1016
35. Chairman, Glavkosmos, 9, Krasnoproletarskya UL, 10 30 30, Moscow

their Escrow Account in India. The proposal, if implemented, would have made KELTEC a public limited company with Board-level participation for Glavkosmos and a full- time Directorship.

- On the same day, i.e., 8 January 1993, Sudhakar sent a letter to Aleksey Vasin[36], referring to his earlier letter dated 13 October 1992 about a proposal for a thousand million rupees-joint venture for the manufacture of cryo engines at KELTEC, and wanted to know *"how soon we can start our joint venture programme for the manufacture of cryo engine at KELTEC."*
- On 29 March 1993, V. Sudhakar sent a letter[37] to Aleksey Vasin requesting him to send urgently his *"proposal in writing either by telex or fax to Prof U.R. Rao, Chairman, ISRO, and a copy to Dr A.E. Muthunayagam, Director, LPSC, Valiamala and myself"* since *"Dr Muthunayagam has indicated to Mr Chandrasekhar (representative of Glavkosmos in India) that he would be happy to entrust the entire work of cryo fabrication to KELTEC provided Glavkosmos and its associated bring all required equipment as part of their investment."*
- In his reply to Sudhakar, Vasin in his fax message sent to KELTEC at 0471-77325 said, *"I inform you that the possibility to deliver machines and equipment is under consideration of Russian government. It will take three months more. I expect to discuss the future trends of our business during my stay in India."*

In the last correspondence, it is essential to note the tone of the letter and the timing mentioned. Because Glavkosmos, by that time, had got a clear picture that the agreement would be scraped and that

36. D.O. No. KELTEC/ B6—5/1015
37. D.O. NO.KELTEC/B6-5/ 1052/92

it was only a question of time. As Vasin feared, Russia cancelled the agreement invoking *force majeure* in less than four months.

It is critically important to note that copies of the correspondence between Glavkosmos and KELTEC were marked to the Chairman, ISRO. This has to be viewed against the backdrop that there was an understanding that after his retirement as Chairman of ISRO, Prof U.R. Rao would take the mantle of KELTEC.

The tie-up was his brainchild.

8

Plot Espionage

The illegal and clandestine operation was clinically and meticulously planned to mislead the US spies in Russia. One such statement made by Glavkosmos, as early as 27 July 1993, was aimed to trick the US by declaring that cryogenic technology had already been transferred to ISRO.

To an interview with *The Christian Science Monitor*, Glavkosmos spokesman Nikolai Semyonov asserted that the company "has already completed the transfer of about 80% of the technology involved. Now they are ready to produce."

It meant, the cargo, as part of the technology transfer should have reached India before 27 July 1993.

S. Nambi Narayanan would also have us believe the version of the Glavkosmos spokesperson when he airs the view (in some recent television interviews, including Asianet News) that the Url flights to India were carrying materials that were part of a legally valid technology transfer. He gives a new twist to the story by adding that ISRO got the whole process advanced with the full co-operation of Glavkosmos to pre-empt the US move to stop the transfer of technology.

A reality check would disprove the statements of both, the Glavkosmos spokesperson and Nambi Narayanan.

- ISRO has no records to show that 80% of the cryogenic technology had been transferred from Glavkosmos before 20 July 1993, the date on which Russia cancelled the first agreement.
- ISRO records would show the three Url flights carrying materials, which were part of the clandestine operation, reached Thiruvananthapuram airport on 23 January, 11 March, and 17 July 1994[38], more than six months after the ISRO-Glavkosmos agreement for the transfer of technology was scrapped by Russia, and that they were transported from Thiruvananthapuram International Airport to ISRO without proper customs clearance.
- If the transportation was advanced, as Nambi Narayanan would have us believe, it should have reached ISRO before July 1993 because the first agreement, which Nambi Narayanan is referring to, was cancelled by Russia on 20 July 1993. The first Url flight carrying materials, as part of the technology transfer, reached India only on 11 January 1994; almost six months after the agreement was cancelled.
- If 80 percent of the cryogenic technology had been transferred from Glavkosmos, as the spokesperson of Glavkosmos would have us believe, then the transportation would have happened before 27 July 1993, the date on which the spokesperson's statement had appeared in The Christian Science Monitor.

D. Sasikumaran, the ISRO-technocrat who was in charge of the transportation part of the cryogenic technology, nails the lies aired by both Nikolai Semyonov and Nambi Narayanan in an interview given to Kaumudi Channel, a Malayalam TV channel. "It was not possible for us to airlift anything from any of the five

38. Read, without proper legal documents

airports in Moscow, tricking the US surveillance. So we had to transport materials to Tashkent airport, using trucks, and airlift to Thiruvananthapuram. We got full co-operation from Glavkosmos. In my opinion, it was a smart operation. And, it was all done after the 1991 Glavkosmos-ISRO agreement was cancelled."

D. Sasikumaran's statement has six crucial elements in it.

- One, certain materials, as part of the technology transfer, were transported from Glavkosmos to ISRO.
- Two, it was not possible to airlift materials from Moscow because of the US surveillance.
- Three, the materials were stealthily transported from Glavkosmos in Moscow to Tashkent in Uzbekistan through road in trucks, covering 3,376 km in 47 hours, from where they were airlifted to Thiruvananthapuram in Url flights that were coming from Moscow.
- Four, the ISRO team got all co-operation from the Russian side.
- Five, the entire operation was done after the 1991 agreement was cancelled.
- Six, it means transportation using Url aviation that he claims to be smart was an illegal act, done clandestinely, after the first agreement was cancelled in July 1993.

The concocted stories by the Glavkosmos spokesperson and Nambi Narayanan have to be read along with the fact that the first cryogenic stage, as per the revised agreement signed between the two parties in January 1994, was to reach India only in 1996.

The US spies knew what was happening. But they could not have physically stopped it. When asked by *The Christian Science Monitor* about the possibility of 80% of the technology already being transferred to India, a US diplomat replied: "the cryogenic booster engines cannot be completed without the remaining technology."

▼

All this while, the CIA was waiting for the right time to throw a spanner into the operations of ISRO when Mariam Rasheeda was arrested by Kerala Police on 20 October 1994, allegedly for overstaying and having developed secretive contacts with D. Sasikumaran, Deputy Director (Fabrication) of the Cryogenic Technology Division of ISRO.

That Sasikumaran was the man in charge of the cryogenic transfer from Glavkosmos to ISRO and that he had developed some unholy relations with a Maldivian woman was the entry point the CIA had been looking for.

To keep the transfer of the "remaining technology" on tenterhooks, the CIA crafted an absurd espionage story theory using the same Url flights, but changing the course of their destination. The CIA gave a 180-degree turn to the flights and aired the story that certain ISRO technocrats had spied the cryogenic missile technology to Pakistan through Url Aviation.

The sole intention of embroiling ISRO and its technocrat in an espionage theory, which any person holding a position in ISRO would otherwise dismiss as absurd, was to ignite a media explosion and bring the hitherto progress in the transfer of technology to sub-zero.

The CIA knew that ISRO didn't have cryogenic technology in 1994, so there was no question of spying the technology to Pakistan: ISRO was not manufacturing missiles (missiles were developed in DRDO); the Url flights from Russia were coming to India, and that technology could not be transferred using two semi-literate women.

A statement by the ISRO Chairman that the organization didn't have cryogenic technology in 1994 would have sealed the fate of the spy story on day one itself.

But the CIA was sure the Chairman wouldn't dare to open his mouth to burst the absurd espionage theory because ISRO would then have to come out clean about the failed illegal attempt to get the same rocket technology transferred to ISRO.

Through this absurd espionage story, the CIA could halt the effective transfer of technology, silence ISRO, and implicate the ISRO-technocrats involved in the clandestine operation – all in one go. Url Aviation didn't bring materials after its third flight in July 1994 because before the ISRO-technocrats could organize the fourth flight scheduled in November 1994, the ISRO spy case had hit the headlines.

How to implicate Glavkosmos and Aleksey Vasin, who was a party to the illegal operation – especially after Russia had ensured the US that cryogenic technology would not be transferred to ISRO and in return Russia had received an economic package from the US – was the next concern for the CIA.

This mission was accomplished by airing another espionage story in which Aleksey Vasin was presented as a sort of middleman. The storyline reads like this – S. Nambi Narayanan and D. Sasikumaran spied the drawings and sketches of Vikas engine to Aleksey Vasin, as part of a trade that would see Vasin sell the documents to three or four third world countries for a price, which they would share between them.

This time also, the CIA was sure ISRO wouldn't utter a word against this absurd theory because Vikas is the indigenously developed liquid propellant system from the French Viking engine, the technology of which was legally transferred to India in 1977.

Why should Aleksey Vasin buy drawings, sketches and documents from ISRO to resell them to other countries when Russia has its liquid propellant system, which is far more superior to the French Viking?

The CIA found that implicating Raman Srivastava in the espionage case would give more credibility to the story since the media had already pictured him as the kingpin of the espionage case. So, Srivastava, though not connected to ISRO or the technocrats in any way, was pictured as an important member of the spy ring.

▼

Certain incidents in ISRO that had nothing to do with the spy case, however, gave a fillip to the master brains behind the espionage story and added credence to the spy story.

Hardly ten days before the media had linked D. Sasikumaran's name to Mariam Rasheeda and labelled him a spy, there was a war of words between him and Sen Gupta IAS, Joint Secretary, Department of Space, at a meeting, chaired by Dr A.E. Muthunayagam, Director of Liquid Propellant Systems Centre (LPSC).

A fifteen-member committee constituted to shortlist two companies from a list of six – L&T, Godrej, MTAR, WIL, KELTEC and HAL – had been dragging their feet for months since the members couldn't take a collective decision. The reason was simple, yet complex. There was a strong lobby in the committee favouring P. Ravindra Reddy of MTAR (who was one of the Directors of Antrix Corporation, owned by the Government of India and administratively controlled by the Department of Space for marketing space products and services, including consultancy services).

Sasikumaran felt the dual role of P. Ravindra Reddy as a Director and contractor difficult to chew and put on record his objections against MTAR, causing great embarrassment to many committee members. Sen Gupta felt Sasikumaran was unnecessarily complicating the issue, especially after ISRO Chairman had expressed his displeasure over the committee's failure to come to an agreed view.

"You don't know anything about technology," Sasikumaran said, pointing his fingers towards Sen Gupta, who lost his cool and retorted, "You may be a great technocrat, but the problem is, you cannot take decisions. That's why projects get delayed."

Sasikumaran was in no mood to spare Gupta. "You bureaucrat, you don't know the nut and bolt of rocketry. Don't try to dictate terms to a technocrat." Gupta felt insulted.

A few days later, when the media commented on D. Sasikumaran's relations with a Maldivian woman, a spy, Sen Gupta found it the right time to drive home the point that it is the bureaucrat who always bridles a technocrat. He transferred Sasikumaran from a highly sensitive post in the Cryogenic Unit in Thiruvananthapuram to Space Application Centre, Ahmedabad, giving credence to newspaper reports that D. Sasikumaran was a member of the spy ring operating from the Liquid Propulsion Systems Centre (LPSC).

▼

Since Mariam Rasheeda was found to be overstaying and had developed contacts with D. Sasikumaran who had visited her in her hotel room at least twice, Kerala police alerted IB about the same on 15 October 1994.

As per the confidential letter[39] signed and sent by V.R. Rajeevan IPS, Commissioner of Police, Thiruvananthapuram City, to K.S. Balasubramanian, DIG of Police (CID) Thiruvananthapuram with copies marked to the DGP, Kerala, and Raman Srivastava, IG of Police (South Zone): officers of Kerala Police, IB and RAW questioned

39 No. SB/1053/G1/94-TC, dated 24 October 1994

Mariam Rasheeda and her friend Fauziya Hassan, another Maldivian woman, on 16 and 19 October.

The letter by the police commissioner reads:

> *On 20.10.94 we got information that some of the press persons had come to know about the matter. Under the above circumstances, I discussed the matter with R.B. Sreekumar, Dy. Director of IB, and told him if they wanted to detain her (Mariam Rasheeda) further, proper legal proceedings have to be initiated against her.*
>
> *Though they were not in a position to rule out the possibilities of Mariam Rasheeda being used for some sort of espionage activities, it was informed that they did not have any evidence to prove any offence... I, therefore, suggested that some more time will be available for them (IB) for further probe if she is proceeded against under the Foreigners Act. This was agreed to by Sreekumar also...*
>
> *I issued instructions to Special Branch Inspector to get a case registered against the foreign national... Confidential enquiries made by this unit have not brought out any facts indicating any espionage activities on the part of this foreigner (Mariam Rasheeda). At the same time, the fact remains that she had contacted a Senior Scientist of Vikram Sarabhai Space Centre (VSSC) on several occasions and it is for the officials of the IB and RAW to make further enquiries regarding this aspect. We have orally requested the IB officials to inform us whether they want the remand period of Mariam Rasheeda to be extended or not. However, they have not given any definite reply to date. In case they do not wish to proceed further with enquiries, we are planning to chargesheet the case against her under the Foreigners Act/rules.*

The police registered crime no. 225/94 against Mariam Rasheeda[40]. She was arrested on 20 October 1994 and was sent to judicial custody the next day.

For a few days to follow, the media brought out explosive stories about the espionage; some stories fed to them by Kerala Police and IB, while some were the exclusives brought out by the investigative journalists.

Kerala Kaumudi continuously reported the spy case and the nexus of Raman Srivastava IPS with the spies. The sleazy stories about Mariam Rasheeda – who was compared to Mata Hari, the Dutch spy – churned out by newspapers charged the socio-political environment of Kerala with the zeal to know more about spies and espionage. A highly responsible *vox populi* offered more and more spicy, sleazy stories on the spies that reached them through dreams in the hangover hours of the highly 'spirited' journalistic crusade.

The CIA left no time to alert its moles in IB. M.K. Dhar, Joint Director of IB, air-dashed to Thiruvananthapuram.

---

40. Under Section 14 of the Foreigners Act, 1946 and Paragraph 7 of the Foreigners Order, 1948

9

Acting under Dictation

Acting under dictation is bad in law – meaning invalid, void, not legally correct. A decision-maker must personally exercise a discretion conferred on him by statute, unless the statute expressly or by implication authorizes another to give binding directions. The decision-maker must not act upon the dictation of another person, be that person a superior officer or even the minister leading the department.

Then what about the Kerala Police acting under the dictation of IB, right from the stage of registering the ISRO espionage case?

Tow Confidential letters – one by Director IB and the other by Thiruvananthapuram City Police Commissioner – prove that certain officers in the Kerala Police, including the DGP, were acting under the dictation of the IB officials, who have or never had any supervisory or other control over Kerala Police. Legally also, IB could not indulge in the investigation of a crime. More importantly, the IB Director had been officially informing these illegal acts to the Principal Secretary to the Prime Minister, Union Home Minister, Cabinet Secretary and Union Home Secretary, regularly.

The unofficial note[41] dated 21.11.1994 sent by the Director of IB to the Cabinet Secretary, Home Minister, Principal Secretary to the Prime Minister and Home Secretary reads:

41. UO Note No.303.DIB/DESP/94

DGP, Kerala had been requested to enlarge the structure of the case (ISRO espionage case) registered under sections 3 and 4 of the Official Secrets Act.

Confidential Letter[42] signed by V.R. Rajeevan IPS, Commissioner of Police, Thiruvananthapuram City, makes it clear that IB officials had interrogated Mariam Rasheeda and Fauziya Hassan on two occasions before Mariam Rasheeda was arrested. *(The letter has been quoted in the previous chapter.)*

The letters tell volumes that IB, a civilian body with no legal power to investigate a crime or interrogate an accused, had given directions to Kerala Police even in matters of registering a case and in enlarging the structure of the case. It had also interrogated the accused before arrest. More worrisome is the fact that those in the highest echelons of power were fully aware of these illegal acts.

The course of action in the espionage case was designed, directed and controlled by IB officials. With M.K. Dhar (Joint Director of IB) taking command of the Thiruvananthapuram office of IB, the scenario underwent a sea change. More names began to appear at regular intervals in all leading newspapers, simultaneously, as if they were briefed by the same source.

It was IB that cast the dramatis personae. Names of S. Nambi Narayanan, Project Director, Cryogenic Systems; D. Sasikumaran, Dy. Project Director, (Fabrication); Aleksey V. Vasin, in charge of Cryogenic Technology in Glavkosmos; and K. Chandrasekhar, the liaison man of Glavkosmos, came in quick succession. Mariam Rasheeda and Fauziya Hassan were cast even before the plot was set. Raman Srivastava had to be cast because *Kerala Kaumudi* had already labelled him as the kingpin. His exclusion could have raised many

42 No. SB/1053/G1/94-TC, dated 24 October 1994

eyebrows. And S.K. Sharma, a labour contractor who didn't know even the full form of ISRO when he was arrested, was miscast.

Meanwhile, Inspector Vijayan had handed over Mariam Rasheeda to IB, allowing himself to be reduced to the role of a peon doing sundry jobs for IB. Occasionally, he got an opportunity to threaten her, or even torture her. IB directed the Kerala Police to bring Fauziya Hassan from Bangalore by force, which they did.

On 13 November 1994, Vanchiyoor Police Station filed an FIR before the local court[43] with Fauziya Hassan as first and Mariam Rasheeda as the second accused. The FIR under Sections 3 and 4 of the Indian Official Secrets Act 1923, read with Section 34 of IPC thus formed the genesis of the espionage case.

Two days later, both the cases (225/94 and 246/94) were handed over to an SIT of Kerala Police headed by Siby Mathews IPS, who was the then DIG of Crime Branch.

It is clear that the moles in IB had planted certain theories tutored by the CIA through Kerala Police officers who willingly accepted to act under the dictation of IB. Kerala Police had absolutely no idea of technology transfer, something they were investigating. They were only carrying out the instructions of the IB.

▼

Beginning with the history of the rocket to the final stage of evolving the know-why from the know-how, the transfer of rocket technology is complex and includes basic conceptual design, fabrication drawings, assembly drawings, assembly procedure, test details during assembly, acceptance criteria, non-conformances during fabrication, spare parts supply, performance in the test-bed (including failure), test result analysis, modifications effected,

43. FIR No. 246/94

flight data, flight failures, metallurgical details of the alloys, the fabrication process, on-the-job training and participation in critical reviews.

To cite an example from ISRO itself, the ISRO technocrats spent nearly 135 man-years in France before the technology of the Viking engine, using the liquid propellant system, was transferred to India under a legal contract. It then took seventeen years for the technocrats in ISRO to develop the Vikas engine, employing the Viking technology, and to use it successfully in PSLV.

Coming to the cryo engine, it was on 17 December 1996, a full twenty-six months after the spy scandal broke out that ISRO tested a subscale cryo engine for ten seconds. A subscale is not even a prototype. It is only a micro-miniature, a prelude to the subsequent development of the prototype, and then the engine as such.

Still, the wise men of IB could make the accused 'confess' that S. Nambi Narayanan and D. Sasikumaran had supplied the Cryogenic Missile Technology to Pakistan for a hefty sum. That too through drawings! That too through two semi-literate Maldivian women!

Remember, fabrication and assembly drawings are just one part of the whole process of technology transfer. They are like one rupee in a hundred-rupee note. Without that one rupee, you cannot have the hundred-rupee note. With the one rupee alone, you cannot even dream of a hundred-rupee note.

The whole idea behind the espionage story was to link ISRO with both Url Aviation and Glavkosmos, since the three parties were instrumental in illegally transferring a major part of the cryogenic technology from Glavkosmos, clandestinely, after Russia had scrapped the first ISRO-Glavkosmos agreement for technology transfer invoking *force majeure*.

10

The Contours of a Himalayan Blunder

Case No. 246/94, better known as the espionage case, was a Himalayan blunder – legally, logically and factually.

Legally, Kerala Police made a mockery of law by invoking the Indian Official Secrets Act, 1923. They were applying the highly sensitive and equally infructuous Act, perhaps, for the first time, and didn't understand that the State police have no jurisdiction under the Act even to file a complaint in a case relating to a Central government institution.

The genesis of a case under the Indian Official Secrets Act is a complaint under section 200 of CrPC by the appropriate government (in the case of ISRO, by the Central government) to the competent magistrate who can take cognizance of an offence under the Act. This is a restrictive Clause under section 13(3) of the IOS Act. Section 13(3) of the Act reads:

> *No Court shall take cognizance of any offence under this Act unless upon complaint made by order of, or under authority from, the appropriate Government or some officer empowered by the appropriate Government in this behalf.*

Section 13(5) of the Act defines appropriate government thus:

> *"Appropriate Government" means – (a) in relation to any offences under section 5 not connected with a prohibited place or with a*

foreign power, the State government; and (b) in relation to any other offence, the Central government.

Section 4(2) of the CrPC clarifies that the procedures laid down in a Special Act would prevail upon the CrPC. IOS Act 1923 is a Special Act.

When you read Section 4(2) of CrPC together with Section 13 of the IOS Act, you will understand how ill-read and inexperienced were the Kerala Police officers, including senior IPS officers, to have directed a junior officer to register a case under IOS Act, involving espionage in ISRO, a Central government organization.

The Act stipulates that the Central government alone should evaluate the entire gamut of things before filing a formal complaint with the competent magistrate who can take cognizance of an offence under the Act when the alleged crime is committed in a Central government organization.

The reason is very simple. Only the Central government can judge whether the prosecution of a spy doing espionage for a foreign country would benefit India or cost heavily at the diplomatic level. It is a clause that empowers the Central government to even deport a spy without launching a complaint against him. It is an area of international diplomacy, which is beyond the scope of CrPC. Just put two American or British citizens in the place of the Maldivian women and watch how those countries would have reacted, even if they were spies.

Why did Kerala Police then file the FIR? The answer is that they were made to do so by IB.It could ride piggyback on Kerala Police and execute the arrests of all others executed – sometimes by reason and sometimes by coercion. So when G. Babu Raj raised some doubts before the arrest of S. Nambi Narayanan, the IB officials threatened to arrest him first.

One wonders whether any of the officials in Kerala Police had even seen the Indian Officials Secrets Act after they had invoked it and began to act upon it because in several official records, the Act is mentioned as IOS Act, 1920 where as the Act was passed only in 1923.Needless to say, Kerala Police officials were ignorant of the provisions of the Act.

The wise men of IB were fully aware of the illegality, but their aim was not to initiate prosecution or punish the 'spies'. They knew there were no spies and no espionage. They could paint the accused as spies, thanks to the sheer unprofessionalism among the cops and journalists in Kerala.

Logically, the content of FIR 246/94 was incongruent with the Confidential Letter[44] sent by V.R. Rajeevan IPS, Commissioner of Police, Thiruvananthapuram City, to the Director General of Police. The letter dated 24 October 1994, four days after the arrest of Mariam Rasheeda, reads on Fauziya Hassan thus:

> *Our inquiries have not revealed anything against Smt Fauziya Hassan and there was no overstay in her case. Confidential inquiries made by this unit have not brought out any facts indicating any espionage activities on the part of this foreigner. Under the above circumstances, she had not been detained and she had left for Bangalore.*

The letter makes it clear that the police, IB or RAW had absolutely no doubts about Fauziya Hassan when they allowed her to return to Bangalore on 19 October 1994 after she was subjected to their interrogation on 16 and 19 October. However, she was brought from Bangalore on 11 November 1994, though her arrest was recorded two days later, and was named the first accused in the espionage case.

---

44. No. SB/1053/G1/94-TC

It means Fauziya was in Bangalore for twenty-two days after she was set free, and that's because Kerala Police, IB and RAW did not have an iota of doubt against her.

Will any spy anywhere in the world ever choose to be a sitting duck for more than three weeks after she was questioned by the police and left free?

Nobody would have prevented Fauziya Hassan had she chosen to leave for the Maldives with her daughter immediately after Mariam was arrested. The fact that she didn't leave India after Mariam Rasheeda was arrested and even after the news about the espionage had appeared in newspapers shatters her portrayal as the prime accused in the ISRO spy case.

Factually, the espionage theory was absurd.

The main charge of the espionage was that Cryogenic Missile Technology was spied from ISRO to Pakistan using Url Aviation and the Maldivian women.Let us analyze the charge and see how porous it is to the casual eyes of a layman.

ISRO didn't have cryogenic technology in 1994. The fact being so, how could the ISRO technocrats spy the Cryogenic Missile Technology to Pakistan?

Cryogenic Missile Technology, as stated in the police records, is a technical stupidity. No country in the world has a missile using the cryogenic engine. To quote from the ISRO official website, "cryogenic stage is technically a very complex system compared to solid or earth-storable liquid propellant stages due to its use of propellants at extremely low temperatures and the associated thermal and structural problems. Oxygen liquifies at -183 deg C and Hydrogen at -253 deg C. The propellants, at these low temperatures, are to be pumped using turbo pumps running at around 40, 000 rpm. It also entails complex ground support systems like propellant storage and filling systems, cryo engine and stage test facilities, transportation and handling of cryo fluids and related safety aspects."

More importantly, you need at least forty-eight hours for filling the cryogenic fuel with a specific impulse in the range of 430 seconds. No sensible military management would recommend a war weapon that needs a gestation period of forty-eight hours before the signal for launch and the actual firing in the thick of a war. Missiles mostly have solid propellants which can be assembled and kept ready in the launching pad. You can fire it in five minutes flat.

Again, there is nothing like missile technology. It is the same rocket technology. You fix either a satellite or warhead (it can be nuclear also) inside the nose cone of the rocket. The rocket just carries your payload. The technically absurd terminology labelled ISRO as a missile-fabricating centre. It was intentional. The very same label America and Pakistan have been trying hard all these years to paste on ISRO, stood engraved on it, thanks to IB.

One can argue that the Kerala Police officers were not savvy with the intricacies of rocketry or technology transfer. But, shockingly, the SIT headed by a DIG of Crime Branch was ignorant of the very basis of a criminal investigation – identifying the crime. It is after identifying the crime that investigation is carried out to track the criminal(s).

A casual fact-checking with the ISRO authorities whether ISRO had the cryogenic technology would have revealed that the crime could not have existed in 1994, and it could have sealed the fate of FIR 246/94 on day one itself as "false and baseless"; something the CBI concluded after eighteen months of investigation.

▼

The ISRO leadership didn't show the guts to nail the lies, but allowed the technically absurd spy theory to snowball. They were afraid whether they too would be branded spies since D.C. Pathak, Director of IB, had informed ISRO Chairman K. Kasturirangan that incriminating documents had been seized from the scientists and that the defence secrets were now with IB. The ISRO Chairman was in a fix. The technocrat started disbelieving the scientifically absurd espionage theory.

The message slowly trickled down. IB attempted the same trick with the Defence Research Development Organisation (DRDO). But the then DRDO Chief A.P.J. Abdul Kalam snubbed IB and stated that nothing had been leaked out of DRDO. He also gave an interview to *India Today* (31 December 1994) in which he said, "If people steal designs hoping to build rockets, they are only cheating themselves."

The IB officers never bothered to check the veracity of its espionage theory at any stage. They extended its area of operation to Russia. This time the technical absurdity they aired was that S. Nambi Narayanan and D. Sasikumaran had struck a deal with Aleksey Vasin to sell the drawings of Vikas engine, which in turn had reached Pakistan.

The Economics Crimes Department of the Federal Counter-Intelligence Service questioned Aleksey Vasin about the 'deal'. He denied the charges, saying there was no need to buy drawings of an engine more than twenty years old when his own country had made far more powerful ones.

The action on the part of IB made A.I. Dunayev, Chairman, Glavkosmos, say, "Those who are initiating such inquiries did not have any technical expertise, let alone any idea of the rich legacy of Indo-Russian space cooperation."

Dunayev was wrong. The master brains for which the officials ofIB were working had full knowledge of the cooperation. They just didn't want the cooperation to grow further. It was for this reason that IB implicated Url Aviation based on extorted statements from D. Sasikumaran that drawings and computer charts of Vikas engine were sent to Aleksey V. Vasin by Nambi Narayanan using Raman Srivastava, who used to deliver the secrets to Url Aviation.

Neither Kerala Police nor IB ever tried to prove its spy ring theory. They didn't want to. For instance, D. Sasikumaran was arrested from Ahmedabad on 21 November 1994. But his house was searched only ten days later. S. Nambi Narayanan was arrested on 30 November. But his house was not searched at all until CBI took control of the investigation.

Can you ever think of a police team giving time to the family members of spies to clear every piece of evidence in a relaxed manner, even after the spy was arrested?

The business of IB was over once the stories were leaked to newspapers, either by themselves or through Kerala Police. With even the *Time Magazine* featuring the bunch of lies, the purpose was more than done.

What more, the IB officials didn't have to take the responsibility for fabricating a case and torturing the space scientists. They can always deny that they didn't do any damn thing because legally and technically, IB is a civilian body. It cannot arrest anybody, cannot investigate a case, cannot even question an ordinary person, leave alone interrogate and torture an accused under police custody. It is all illegal. But they did all that. Tortured the accused under police custody, extorted statements from them, video-graphed the forced 'confessions' and, in the process, violated all laws of the land.

Still, the IB officials may go scot-free. They fooled the Kerala Police to that extent. Once they allowed the SIT to enter theIB interrogation report as their own in their Case Diaries, the buck was neatly passed on to the Kerala Police officers.

Part - III

Ghost Organisations

11

Unpacking IB

Still, something remained incomplete. The IB officials couldn't interrogate Raman Srivastava.

G. Babu Raj, Deputy SP had been to Bangalore specifically to identify K.L. Bhasin. He identified the man and collected his photos. They were shown to Fauziya Hassan on 26 November 1994 and she identified the photo as that of the man who was with them at the Army Club in Bangalore.

But Mathew John of IB asked the Dy. SP not to enter the crucial piece of evidence that went against the IB theory in his Case Diary. Instead, Mathew John sent a report to the IB Director on 1 December 1994 stating that Raman Srivastava "had in fact, emerged as the most important member of the inner group of the spy ring."

The same day, Mathew John and R.B. Sreekumar of IB made an unscheduled visit to the office of T.V. Madhusoodanan, DGP. Present in his room were Siby Mathews and G. Babu Raj. The IB officers didn't know Siby Mathews had sent a confidential letter to the DGP the previous day (30 November 1994) requesting him to hand over the case to CBI.

The letter reads:

(1) *The incidents of this case are spread over the three states of Kerala, Tami Nadu, and Karnataka, and foreign locations like Colombo and Male.*

(2) *There is reason to believe that strategically important information about the IAF/Armed Forces (R&D Wing) have been passed on by the espionage chain to unfriendly countries. The complicity of senior military personnel is very likely. The State police may not be able to question them, conduct a search in their office, etc.*

(3) *There is information (not fully authenticated) about the involvement of a senior officer. Due to the above-mentioned reasons, I do not think the Special Team now in charge of the case would be able to do full justice to the case. This is an apt case to be transferred to the Central Bureau of Investigation who are better equipped and also have the advantage of being a Central Police Investigation outfit.*

When Mathew John repeated his demand that Srivastava should be arrested immediately, Siby Mathews reiterated his stand that he could not arrest an IG without any evidence. Mathew John then began a war of words with Siby Mathews and the DGP intervened. The statement was clear. "Enough is enough. Nobody will be arrested without evidence, so long as I am here."

Mathew John, the Joint Director of IB thundered, "There is no evidence against him. And you won't get that also. Still, you have to arrest him. Or else we know how to book him under the National Security Act." Mathew John and Sreekumar stormed out of the DGP's room. In the process, they tumbled down two chairs which they didn't bother to put back in their places.

The wise men of IB then, through their Delhi office, moved the Union Home Ministry to invoke NSA against Srivastava. The officer in Delhi asked for evidence to book a senior IG but the IB men had nothing concrete to give him other than the statements of the accused. Reading the complex issues involved in the move, the officer sought more time.

The same evening, though it was a busy day for Chief Minister K. Karunakaran, he made it convenient for Mathew John and Sreekumar to talk to him at length about the espionage case. They wanted him to direct the DGP to arrest Raman Srivastava immediately. He gave them a patient listening. He didn't say 'Yes'. He didn't say 'No'.

Mathew John then sent his emissaries to the Thiruvananthapuram bureau of *The Indian Express* and leaked to the paper the IB's latest report to its Director, since he had not received a specific reply from the Chief Minister.

▼

2 December 1994

The Indian Express front-paged an exclusive titled 'Net Closing in on Top Police Official'. K. Karunakaran read the report and felt a slight headache. He wanted to get rid of it. He picked up the phone and talked to Margaret Alva, Union Minister for Personnel. The pain subsided. The ISRO espionage case was transferred to the CBI the same day.

The decision came as a bolt from the blue for the IB officers. They never wanted the CBI to probe the case. They knew their cock and bull story would explode in hours.

IB had thwarted an earlier move to transfer the case to CBI. It was in the second week of November, 1994. Following *Kerala Kaumudi's* so-called investigative pieces on Raman Srivastava, the DGP was about to recommend the transfer of the espionage case to CBI when Mathew John and R.B. Sreekumar prevented him. The DGP then talked to IB Director D.C. Pathak over the phone. For reasons best known to Pathak, he advised the DGP to constitute a Special Investigation Team of the Kerala Police instead of transferring the case to CBI.

Why did the Director of IB mislead the DGP?

Why did he advise the DGP to take the wrong path when the State government had absolutely no jurisdiction in a case registered under sections 3, 4, and 5 of the IOS Act involving a Central government organization?

Moreover, only CBI can take the investigation to foreign countries.

Sounds intriguing!

▼

What is the real face of the Intelligence Bureau?

Sarita Rani in a report in *The Wire*, 25 December 2018, details the stranger than fiction face of IB.

> *The IB was born in 1887 through an executive order of the British government, thirty years after the 1857 revolt, to keep the British government "fully informed of everything affecting the public peace and order, which can be made the subject of observation."*
>
> *After the British government dissolved the East India Company and took over its colony in India by the Government of India Act of 1858, the queen appointed her first secretary to India. Like the first secretary, the six others who followed him also had small tenures.*
>
> *In 1886, Richard Assheton Cross was appointed the secretary. Having served Prime Minister Benjamin Disraeli as Home Secretary for six years (1874 to 1880), Cross was specially chosen to make India safe for the British Empire.*
>
> *Within six months of assuming office, Cross wrote a letter, dated 25 March 1887, Secret Dispatch No 11, to the Viceroy's Camp in India.*
>
> *He asked that a system be set up for "collection of secret and political intelligence in India," specifically, any observation*

"with particular reference to the expedience of employing especially qualified natives in those parts of the Empire, notably the Punjab and Hyderabad, which are exceptionally exposed to political intrigues or dangers."

On 15 November 1887, Viceroy Dufferin wrote back to Cross saying he had come up with a scheme to collect intelligence on the natives.

Dufferin enclosed copies of reports from two officers – Colonel Henderson and D.E. McCracken. The plan was two-fold, based on the kind of territories in India at the time.

(a) In British controlled provinces, Dufferin planned to use the services of the police force.

(b) In native ruled princely states, he planned to use "the existing means at the disposal of Political Offices, for the collection of intelligence on political, social and religious movements."

Dufferin believed that Indians would object to the creation of a large British detective force stomping all over the place. Besides, it would defeat the very purpose of stealth. His plan was to ask local governments to collect intelligence for their own purpose and report relevant information to the Government of India.

Remarkably, this continues to be the Intelligence Bureau structure and mandate. To be entirely specific, the Intelligence Bureau's mandate is to collect intelligence on political, social and religious movements in the country on behalf of the state (read, for the party in power at the centre). The subject group includes all politicians of all political parties, dissident political and non-political groups (violent or non-violent), and religious groups that the state wants to keep an eye on.

In today's English, the IB's formal and legal mandate is Opposition Research, spying on dissidents and profiling.

Who does the IB answer to today?

Technically, it is listed as answerable to the Minister of Home Affairs. But, and this is true, there is no Act of the Indian Parliament or executive order relating to the functioning of the IB. This organisation has no charter under Indian law post-Independence. It is a ghost organization.

Worse, this is not unknown to the judiciary.

In 2012, R.N. Kulkarni, a former IB officer, filed a PIL asking the organisation to explain its constitutional or statutory sanction. Kulkarni told the court, "all that the IB has to explain for its evolution over the past 125 years is the British order issued in 1887. Neither the Indian Independence nor the adoption of a Constitution nor even regulatory statutes for Central police organizations, like the CRPF and CISF, ever accorded any legal status to the IB, which exists in a constitutional vacuum."

How can the IB, established under an administrative order without any constitutional or statutory identity even after the commencement of the Constitution in 1950, be permitted to function as an apex national security apparatus, questioned Kulkarni's PIL. This extra-constitutional status infringes upon the rights of citizens as well as those serving in the IB, the PIL added (*Times of India*, 26 March 2012).

When the court asked the Centre to explain its position, the Central government responded, "The IB is a civilian organisation which does not enjoy police powers."

In 2017-2018, the Home Ministry continued to acknowledge the lack of legal mandate for IB when the eight President's Police Medal for Distinguished Service and twenty-six Police Medal Meritorious Service for the IB had to be categorised under the Union Home Ministry, instead of a legal intelligence body.

Yet, this hasn't deterred IB officials from pursuing their 'mandate'. In 2012, the same year as India celebrated its 65th Independence anniversary, Intelligence Bureau celebrated its 125th year of founding. It even brought out a special issue to mark the occasion.

IB sees itself as coming from an older tradition than Independent India. At its very core, it pays homage to a set of values that are not compatible with the idea of freedom and liberty. In its very founding, history and tradition, it is anti-freedom.

How could it be different? It was founded to suppress voices against the Empire. See how government after government allows this illegal entity to take any institution or individual in India for granted, throwing to the wind the laws.

Neither the governments nor the courts interfere with IB's activities, even if they are illegal. Even something as serious as interrogating the accused remanded under police custody and torturing them.

It is strange that even S. Nambi Narayanan who has moved the courts – from the Magistrate Court to the Supreme Court, more than once – chose to spare the very same IB officials who tortured him to the extent that he was on the razor's edge for a few hours at the torture centre in the Hindustan Latex Guest House in Thiruvananthapuram.

▼

It is difficult to accept that some of the top brass of IB worked as CIA's moles and sabotaged India's potential share in the space market. But then, you have to view it against the backdrop of the Rattan Sehgal episode. Sehgal, with twenty-eight years of experience in the IB, was to become its Director following Arun Bhagat's retirement when the Central government sacked him as

Additional Director. Subsequently, he was put under house arrest in December 1996.

A report in *India Today* (15 March 1997) by Charulatha Joshi reads:

> *On the face of it, the charges against Sehgal seem serious enough. He had "nine unauthorised and clandestine" meetings with station chief of the CIA, Timothy Long, and his deputy Susan Brown of the US embassy in India between September 19 and October 31, 1996, in Sehgal's Bharati Nagar residence and in the parking lot of Ambassador Hotel in Delhi. On September 18 last year, he received a large packet from Ms August, the former Deputy Station Chief of the CIA, outside Ambassador Hotel.*
>
> *Arun Bhagat, Director of IB, stated that "an analysis of the evidence shows that Sehgal was not working for the CIA, but was probably being cultivated by the Americans".*

Why such unauthorized meetings? Is he the only black sheep the IB had or has? A million-dollar question!

Not much is heard of Sehgal since.

▼

Under the head, "collection of secret and political intelligence in India," IB gets a huge allocation in the annual budget that gets enhanced year after year.

This budgeted amount is not audited. IB is not answerable even to the Parliament. It is interesting to see how the three pillars of Indian democracy – Parliament, Executive and Judiciary – view the issue.

Indian Parliament is yet to realize that IB should have a constitutional or statutory identity. The executive doesn't think there should at least be an executive order of the Government of India to justify IB's legal existence. As such IB exists in a constitutional vacuum. And the Judiciary thinks the security of the nation would be threatened if IB is made accountable to the Parliament. India is the only democracy in the world where even the Supreme Court would rule that the intelligence agency need not be accountable to the people or Parliament.

> *The Supreme Court today dismissed a petition that sought to make intelligence agencies like the Intelligence Bureau (IB), the Research & Analysis Wing (RAW) and the National Technical Research Organization (NTRO) accountable to Parliament, saying that getting into the domain of intelligence may create a dent in national security.*
>
> *The NGO had submitted in the PIL that the agencies were being misused for political purposes and there was an urgent need to make these organizations accountable to Parliament.*
>
> *On February 1, 2013, advocate Prashant Bhushan, appearing for the NGO, had submitted that India is the only democracy in the world whose intelligence agencies have no legitimacy in the eyes of the law and are not accountable to the people or Parliament.*
>
> *The bench had said it is a policy matter to be decided by the Centre but had agreed to hear the plea after the petitioner contended that earlier also the court had passed directions on policy matters*[45].

---

45. Source: Indiatvnews.com (23 February 2016)

12

Unpacking CBI

Sometime in 2005, Navendra Kumar filed a petition[46] before the High Court of Assam to quash the Resolution[47] that established the CBI as ultra vires the Constitution of India, and to quash the criminal proceedings against him in the Court of Special judge (CBI), Assam, at Guwahati. The court dismissed the petition on 30 November 2007 and Navendra Kumar appealed against the order.

Before going into the details of the Writ Appeal[48], let us see some facts about the genesis of CBI as shown on its website[49].

> *At an early stage of World War II, the Government of India realised that vast increase in expenditure for war efforts had provided opportunities to unscrupulous and anti-social persons, both officials and non-officials, for indulging in bribery and corruption at the cost of the public and the government. It was felt that police and other law enforcement agencies under the State governments were not in a position to cope with the situation. An executive order was, therefore, passed by the Government of India in 1941, setting up the Special Police Establishment (SPE)*

46. W.P.(C)No.6877of 2005
47. No. 4/31/61-T, dated 01-04-1963
48. No. 119 of 2008
49. https://cbi.gov.in/About-Us

under a DIG in the then Department of War with a mandate to investigate cases of bribery and corruption in transactions with which War and Supply Department of the Government of India was concerned. At the end of 1942, the activities of the SPE were extended to include cases of corruption on Railways also, presumably because the Railways were vitally concerned with movement and supply of war materials.

In 1943, an Ordinance was issued by the Government of India, by which a Special Police Force was constituted and vested with powers for the investigation of certain offences committed in connection with the departments of the Central government committed anywhere in British India. As a need for a Central government agency to investigate cases of bribery and corruption was felt even after the end of the war, the Ordinance issued in 1943, which had lapsed on 30 September 1946, was replaced by the Delhi Special Police Establishment Ordinance of 1946. Subsequently, the same year Delhi Special Police Establishment Act, 1946 was brought into existence.

The CBI website states that it "derives power to investigate from the Delhi Special Police Establishment Act, 1946." But it was precisely this power to investigate and the very question of the legality of CBI that Navendra Kumar challenged through his writ petition and later through a writ appeal.

Justice I.A. Ansari and Justice (Mrs) Indira Shah heard the case on 8 October 2013 and delivered judgment on 6 November 2013. The Bench in unambiguous language held

CBI is neither an organ nor a part of the DSPE and the CBI cannot be treated as a 'police force' constituted under the DSPE Act, 1946. (Para 179) We hereby also set aside and quash the impugned Resolution, dated 01.04.1963, whereby CBI has been constituted. (Para 180)

It is interesting to see that the judgment begins with a quote of Thomas Jefferson, the principal author of the Declaration of Independence (1776) and the third President of the United States, "When the people fear the government, there is tyranny. When the government fears the people, there is liberty." But it set the stage ready for one of the boldest judgments passed by any Court of Appeal in India, and one that didn't get the due attention it deserves.

Excerpts from the judgment[50]

Article 21 is one of the most cherished provisions in our Constitution, which prohibits the State from depriving a person of his life and liberty except according to the procedure established by law. However, what happens if by the State's action, which has been neither sanctioned by legislation nor has been taken in valid exercise of its executive powers, the ineffaceable mandate of Article 21 gets smudged.

This is precisely the issue, which the appellant has been, for almost a decade of litigation, urging the court to decide. Having been unsuccessful in his attempt to convince the court in his writ petition of the correctness and righteousness of his contentions, the appellant is, now, before us, seeking a revisit to his submissions. *(Paragraph 2)*

Some of the prominent questions, which have arisen for determination in this appeal, are:

(i) *Whether Central Bureau of Investigation, popularly called CBI, is a constitutionally valid police force empowered to investigate crimes?*

(ii) *Could a police force, empowered to investigate crimes, have been created and constituted by a mere Resolution of Ministry*

---

50. W. A. No. 119 OF 2008 IN W. P. (C) No. 6877 OF 2005, dated 6 November 2013

of Home Affairs, Government of India, in purported exercise of its executive powers?

(iii) *Could a police force constituted by a Home Ministry Resolution arrest a person accused of committing an offence, conduct search and seizure, submit a charge-sheet, and/or prosecute an alleged offender?*

(iv) *Whether CBI is a police force constituted under the Union's Legislative powers conferred by List 1 Entry 8?*

(v) *Do Entry 1 and 2 of the Concurrent List empower the Union Government to raise a police force and that, too, by way of Executive instructions of Union Home Ministry?*

(vi) *Whether Delhi Special Police Establishment Act, 1946 empowers the Union Home Ministry to establish a 'police force' in the name of CBI?*

(vii) *Above all, is it permissible for the Executive to create a police force with power to investigate crimes in exercise of its executive powers, when exercising of such a power adversely affects or infringes fundamental rights embodied in Part III of the Constitution, particularly, Article 21? (Para 2.a)*

The constitutional validity of the formation of the CBI and its powers to investigate and functions as a police force and/or its powers to prosecute an offender were challenged in the writ petition, by contending that CBI is not a statutory body, the same having been constituted not under any statute, but an Executive Order/ Resolution[51].

On the other hand, the police is a State subject within the scheme of the Constitution of India since it is only a State legislature, which, in terms of Entry No. 2 of List-II (State List) of the Seventh Schedule

51. No. 4/31/61-T, dated 01-04- 1963, of the Ministry of Home Affairs, Government of India

to the Constitution of India is competent to legislate on the subject of police and, therefore, the Central government could not have taken away the power, which so belongs to State Legislatures, and create or establish an investigating agency, in the name of CBI, adversely affecting or offending the fundamental rights, guaranteed under Part 111 of the Constitution of India (Para 4- iv).

To substantiate the above contention, reliance was placed on the Constituent Assembly debates, dated 29-08-1949, wherein Dr B.R. Ambedkar had clarified that the word 'investigation', appearing in Entry 8 of List I (Union List) of the Seventh Schedule, which read: *Central Bureau of Intelligence and Investigation, would not permit making of an 'investigation' into a crime by the Central government in as much as investigation would be constitutionally possible only by a police officer under the CrPC, police being exclusively a State subject and the word 'investigation', appearing in Entry 8 of List I (Union List), would, in effect, mean making of merely an enquiry and not investigation into a crime as is done by a police officer under the Code of Criminal Procedure. The word investigation is, therefore, according to the Constituent Assembly Debates, intended to cover general enquiry for the purpose of finding out what is going on and such an investigation is not an investigation preparatory to the filing of a charge-sheet against an offender, because it is only a police officer, under the Criminal Procedure Code, who can conduct 'investigation'. (Para 4-v)*

In the writ petition, the Union of India did not file any response. But CBI, as respondent no. 2, filed an affidavit, wherein it claimed that it had been exercising functions and powers of the police under the Delhi Special Police Establishment Act, 1946. The CBI further submitted that the CBI has been functioning for more than four decades, but its constitutional validity has never been challenged by anyone and, hence, this settled position may not be unsettled.

Report of the Amicus Curiae

Mr N. Dutta, learned *amicus curiae*, has submitted that the impugned Resolution, dated 01-04-1963, clearly shows that CBI has been constituted for achieving six specified purposes as have been mentioned in the Resolution itself. Till date, no statute has been enacted by Parliament establishing a body called CBI.

Since there is no legislation constituting CBI, its Constitutional validity, according to the learned amicus curiae has to be tested in the light of the provisions embodied in the Constitution of India. (Para 18)

CBI and DSPE are not the same things, but everybody appears to have proceeded on the basis that they are the same. Whereas DSPE has been established under the DSPE Act 1946, CBI – points out the amicus curiae – has been constituted by a mere executive fiat. (Para 19)

It has been further submitted by the learned amicus curiae that though the CBI has been empowered under the impugned Resolution, dated 01.04.1963, to *investigate* crimes, no power has been specifically provided for *prosecution* of offenders by the CBI. In fact, points out the learned amicus curiae, even under the DSPE Act, 1946, DSPE can merely *investigate* a case and lay charge-sheet and, hence, the CBI's role shall come to an end once *investigation* is complete. (Para 20)

It has been pointed out by the learned amicus curiae that in terms of Section 36 of the CrPC, police officers superior in rank to an officer-in-charge of a police station, may exercise the same powers, throughout the local area to which they are appointed, as may be exercised by such officer within the limits of his station. Under Section 2(c) of the DSPE Act, 1946, a member of the DSPE may, subject to any order, which the Central government may make in this behalf, exercise any power of the officer-in-charge of a police station in the area, which he is, for the time being, posted to. When exercising the powers, he shall be subject to any such orders, which may be made by the Central government and be deemed to be an officer-in-charge of a police station discharging the function of an officer within the limits of his station.

If the expression, 'Officer in charge of a police station', appearing in Section 2(c) of the DSPE Act, 1946, is read together with Section 36 of the CrPC, it would become clear that an officer of the DSPE, while functioning in any State, shall be subordinate to the superior officers of the State police. Whereas, in the case of CBI, while investigating a case in any State, by virtue of its powers under Section 5 read with Section 6 of the DSPE Act, 1946, the CBI investigators report to their own hierarchy of officers and not to the superior police officers of the police station within whose local jurisdiction he may be investigating a case. (Para 22)

Queries Raised by the Court

After hearing the parties as well as the learned amicus curiae, this court raised the following queries:

- If a pre-constitutional law was made on a subject, which is now covered by State List, whether the law will be valid after the Constitution has come into force, bearing in mind Article 372?
- Whether a law made by the Parliament, on a subject covered by the State List, be valid in respect of a Union Territory, after the Constitution has come into force?
- The Executive power of the State is co-extensive with its legislative power. Is it, therefore, possible to constitute an investigating agency by a State taking recourse to State's executive power?
- Delhi was a Part-C State under the Government of India Act. On coming into force of the Constitution, it was made a Union Territory and it now enjoys the status of a State, but some of

its powers under the State List are exercised by the Parliament. The Court wants to know details of the legislative history of the present status of Delhi, as a State, and its legislation-making process. (Para 23)

The point that now falls for determination is whether CBI is established under the DSPE Act 1946, or is an organ of the DSPE Act. (Para 28)

No. 4/31/61-
Government of India Ministry of Home Affairs
New Delhi, the 1st April 1963

RESOLUTION

The Government of India has had under consideration the establishment of a Central Bureau of Investigation for the investigation of crimes at present handled by the Delhi Special Police Establishment, including especially important cases under the Defence of India Act and Rules, particularly of hoarding, black-marketing, and profiteering in essential commodities, which may have repercussions and ramifications in several states; the collection of intelligence relating to certain types of crimes; participation in the work of the National Central Bureau connected with the International Criminal Police Organization; the maintenance of crime statistics and dissemination of information relating to crime and criminals; the study of the specialized crime of particular interest to the Government of India or crimes having all-India or interstate ramifications or of particular importance from the social point of view; the conduct of Police research, and the coordination of laws relating to crime. As the first step in that direction, the Government of India decided to set up with effect

> *from 1 April 1963 a Central Bureau of Investigation at Delhi with the following six divisions, namely: Investigation and Anti-corruption Division; Technical Division; Crime Records and Statistics Division; Research Division; Legal Division & General Division, and Administrative Division. (Para 33)*

On a careful reading of the contents of the impugned Resolution, what becomes evident is that the Resolution does not refer to any provisions of the DSPE Act, 1946 as the source of its power. In other words, deriving strength from the DSPE Act, 1946, the CBI has not been constituted. One cannot, therefore, treat the CBI as an organ or part of the DSPE either. (Para 36)

The learned ASG has completely failed to show that the CBI can be said to have been established or constituted as an organ or part of the DSPE or is a special force, which has been constituted by taking recourse to Section 2 of the DSPE Act, 1946. We have, therefore, no hesitation in concluding that CBI is not established under the DSPE Act, 1946, or is an organ of the Delhi Special Police Establishment. (Para 38)

Subject to the validity of the DSPE Act 1946, only Delhi Special Police Establishment can be termed as a statutory body created by the DSPE Act, 1946, and not the CBI. (Para 43)

This Court, vide order dated 20.01.2013, has directed the respondents to produce the records relating to the creation of the CBI. It is relevant to note that despite directions, the respondents did not file the original records; rather they produced a certified copy of the records received from the National Archives. (Para 45)

However, even perusal of the entire records makes it clear that the Resolution was neither produced before the President of India nor did it ever receive the assent of the President of India. Hence, strictly speaking, this Resolution cannot even be termed as the decision of the Government of India. (Para 46)

While we decline to hold and declare that the DSPE Act, 1946, is not a valid piece of legislation, we do hold that the CBI is neither an organ nor a part of the DSPE and the CBI cannot be treated as a 'police force' constituted under the DSPE Act, 1946. (Para 179)

We hereby also set aside and quash the impugned Resolution, dated 01.04.1963, whereby CBI has been constituted. (Para 180)

▼

The judgment of 6 November 2013 declared that CBI was not a legal entity. The Union government that hadn't otherwise bothered to file an affidavit in the case sprung into action, moved to court, and obtained a stay order in three days.

A report by *India Today online* dated 9 November 2013 reads:

The Supreme Court on Saturday stayed a Gauhati High court verdict which had declared the setting up of the Central Bureau of Investigation (CBI) as unconstitutional. "There shall be a stay of operation of the impugned judgment of Nov 6, 2013, passed by Gauhati High Court," said the apex court bench of Chief Justice of India P. Sathasivam and Justice Ranjana Desai, after hearing a plea from the Central government against the verdict.

The Supreme Court observed that the judgment had to be stayed since the accused in two sensational cases have sought a stay of the trial. The apex court also has issued notice to the petitioner Navendra Kumar on whose plea the Gauhati High Court passed the judgment and posted the matter for hearing on December 6.

The apex court also refused the preliminary objection that the Department of Personnel and Training was not authorised to file an appeal in the matter.

"We will consider and go through the appeal filed by the Centre," said the court.

"We are concerned with all other CBI cases," said the court.

Attorney General G.E. Vahanvati had told the court that the Gauhati High Court's reasoning that the DSPE Act did not apply to the CBI was a convoluted logic.

The matter was heard by Chief Justice P. Sathasivam at his residence. In its appeal, the government had sought an urgent hearing against the High Court order saying it "directly impacts about 9,000 trials currently underway and about one thousand investigations which are being undertaken by the CBI."

The Special Leave Petition settled by Vahanvati said, "If the impugned order is not stayed, it will frustrate the law machinery and may result in multiplicity of proceedings." "The order is already being seized upon by various accused persons in various proceedings in the country to seek a stay of further proceedings against them," the petition drawn by advocate Devadatt Kamat said.

The Centre also contended that the High Court has erred in holding that the constitution of CBI was illegal, that the Resolution constituting it needed Presidential assent and that it could not be treated as a police force.

▼

Since 13 November 2013, CBI has been on a legal ventilator. It is sad that the much-trumpeted India's premier investigating agency and a member of the Interpol is surviving on the support of a stay order.

Neither the Executive, nor the Legislature, nor the Judiciary who are accountable to the citizens has shown keen interest to undo the legal stalemate of CBI. The Parliament has done little; the executive loves to meddle with the confusion; the judiciary pretends to be oblivious of a case of paramount importance that has been pending decision for the past eight years; and the media is happy majoring in on minor things even as more and more criminal cases are being transferred to CBI – one of the latest cases being to investigate who all conspired to effectuate the illegal arrest of S. Nambi Narayanan in the ISRO espionage case and tortured him.

"Collectively, we are making a mockery of the judicial system," the Supreme Court said, referring to the sheer number of trivial and miscellaneous cases that have prevented the top court from deciding the ones that really matter to those waiting for final decisions of their long-pending matters (*Hindustan Times*, 4 August 2021).

If what the Supreme Court said was self-criticism with utmost honesty and integrity, why doesn't the Apex Court decide on the question of the legality of both IB and CBI and pass orders if the Court, in its wisdom, thinks both the cases are not "trivial and miscellaneous?" The verdict would make criminal investigation and prosecution in our country more credible, transparent, responsible and sensible.

In the absence of such an order, today we are witnessing a weird context of criminal investigation in which the CBI[52] is investigating the illegality in the arrest of S. Nambi Narayanan, one of the six accused in the ISRO espionage case of 1994, against eighteen persons, including eleven officers of IB (IB doesn't have even the string of a stay order from any court in India to hang on to) under ten sections of IPC, even as the registration of the espionage case by the Kerala Police (246/94) and its re-registration by the CBI[53] both under the Indian Official Secrets Act, 1923, were illegal.

"The problem in India is that both the law enforcement and intelligence organizations do not have a sound legal basis." (Manish Tewari, *The Hindu*, 21 July 2021)

52. Legal basis of the CBI hangs on a stay order from the Supreme Court the Government of India had obtained in 2013
53. RC.11(S)/1994-CBI/SIU.VI/SIC.II

Part - IV

The Breakthrough

13

Interlude

Nambi Narayanan woke up from a deep sleep.

He had no idea of the time and space. He only knew he had slept for years. He felt as if he was floating. The pain was not there. He put his legs on the floor. They didn't ache. He touched his toes. They had stopped bleeding.

There were a few faces around him. All blurred. He could not identify anyone. Then he heard someone asking him about his first meeting with a woman called Mariam Rasheeda.

In no time, he sensed the space and pulsed the time. It was the same Hindustan Latex Guest House in Thiruvananthapuram.

He knew the character he had to play – the spy.

He recognized the blurred faces – the wise men of IB.

He felt he should kill them one by one. He felt a tornado whirling inside. He felt his arms had become swords and legs as strong and powerful as that of a leviathan. He stood up and cried for blood. He roamed around in the room with his swords stretched out. He hit against a man. He was about to plunge his swords into his belly. But then, changed his decision. He wanted to chop his head. He wanted to see blood gushing out like a fountain from his neck. So he looked at the man's face. It was Mr F.

The tornado settled. The swords became arms.

"I believe and trust you. I don't want to kill you," he said to Mr F. In the next moment, he fell asleep like a log of wood.

The log was reborn as a plant the next morning. He looked at the calendar – 4 December.

Mr C was all smiles. "We have understood your version that rocketry cannot be spied through documents. But, have you understood our version?" he asked.

"Yes," said he.

"Can you repeat that, please? I mean our version. We just want to know whether you have understood our version the way we have understood your version."

Nambi Narayanan became alert. There was a tone of pleading in Mr C's voice. Could this be a trap?

He noticed a blue telephone on the teapoy in front of him. Why is this phone here, he wondered. Also, he felt the teapoy was an odd place for the telephone, especially when the room had a table. Again, who would keep a phone in the interrogation room?

In a flash, he got the clue. Bugging. The interrogators want their version in his voice. He smiled inside and cleared his throat.

"I was approached by one Habibullah for spying documents to Pakistan. It was in 1982..." Nambi Narayanan took a pause and looked at the IB men. He saw their faces blooming. He continued, "1982... Is that not the year you have told me?"

Nambi Narayanan took another pause and looked at the IB men. The bloom on their faces had faded.

Suddenly, someone dashed in. "Let's get ready. We have to move," he said.

"Please give us another fifteen minutes," Mr A was pleading.

"Sorry, they have already called thrice. If you don't move now, you will have to face the consequence. You know how these guys can react."

"OK. Let's go," said Mr C. "Nambi, please remember that you should tell more or less in line with our version to those who are now going to question you. Otherwise, we won't be able to help you."

Nambi Narayanan didn't answer. He was wondering who would be the new interrogators. Any other hell is better than this hell. Any other devil is better than Mr A, he tried to console himself.

He heard something being thrown down. He turned back. Mr A was shivering with fury. The blue telephone was not on the teapoy. Its broken pieces lay scattered on the mosaic floor. Nambi Narayanan focussed his eyes on the floor to catch the bugging equipment. But, before he could track it, someone pulled him out of the room.

Mr D came, took his hands, and said, "Good luck!"

Nambi Narayanan looked around. He was searching for someone he didn't know.

▼

When the CBI team led by M.L. Sharma, Joint Director and Special Inspector General of Police, took the reins of investigation on 4 December 1994, the Special Investigation Team (SIT) leader handed over the espionage script to CBI along with the statements of IB and Kerala Police.

The storyline goes like this.

- S. Nambi Narayanan and D. Sasikumaran, senior technocrats of ISRO, had passed documents/drawings relating to Vikas engine technology, cryo technology and PSLV flight data to Pakistan.
- K. Chandrasekhar, agent of Glavkosmos, S.K. Sharma, a Bangalore-based businessman, and Raman Srivastava, IG, had passed secret documents from Aeronautical Defence Establishment (ADE) Bangalore, to Pakistan.
- All these documents reached the hands of Mohammed Aslam, a Pakistani nuclear scientist, and Mohammed Pasha in return for cash running into lakhs of American dollars.
- The spies had a financier, Mohiyuddin, Assistant Manager of Habib Bank, in Maldives. Fauziya Hassan, Mariam Rasheeda, Zuheira, and Aleksey V. Vasin were the conduits.

- Important meetings of the spies were held at Madras, Bangalore and Thiruvananthapuram.

Something odd caught the attention of CBI at the very outset. Statements of the accused, as recorded by SIT, were contradicting; those recorded by IB were contradicting; and that of Kerala Police and IB were contradicting.

In spite of the multiple contradictions, CBI presumed the disclosures were true and began the investigation after taking the records of IB and Kerala Police as the basic raw materials. But a rapid-fire interrogation of the accused by M.L. Sharma revealed one thing – all the statements were made on suggested lines and under duress.

The spy ring theory of the IB-Kerala Police combine lacked authenticity since ISRO had not filed any complaint about losing secret documents.

Interpol, Colombo was pressed into service to dish out evidence against Zuheira, the Maldivian woman settled in Sri Lanka.

The Ministry of Defence and National Security, Maldives, did a thorough investigation about the two Maldivian women.

On its part, CBI left no stone unturned. The top brass, including the Director, interrogated the accused. Modern techniques in crime investigation, including polygraph test, were done on the accused.

14

The Lie Detector

But for the roar of the engine, there was absolute silence as the jeep entered the CRPF camp, Pallipuram, Thiruvananthapuram. The jeep stopped in front of a two-storeyed yellow building.

And, Nambi Narayanan got scared. He had read somewhere that yellow is the colour of lord Brahma's daughter – the blind girl with yellow hair. The goddess of death!

As he alighted from the jeep, his hands were cuffed and he was escorted to a room where a man introduced himself as R.S. Dhankar, Deputy SP of CBI.

"I am the Chief Investigating Officer of the ISRO espionage case," he said and showed his identity card.

Nambi Narayanan remembered that the IB interrogators never revealed their identity. He was then taken to another room furnished with a cot. Darshan Singh, a constable, was posted near him. Sitting on the cot, he took his first lunch since 2 December.

Around 2.30 p.m. a tall, slim, fair man in his late forties with blue eyes and a chiselled nose entered his room, but immediately turned back, as if he had some second thoughts, and walked briskly to the adjacent room, trailing behind him the sound of his footsteps that proclaimed authority.

"You bastard, you have sold the nation to enemies. How do you call yourself an Indian? Forget that you are a scientist."

Nambi Narayanan then heard the voice of his fellow technocrat Sasikumaran from the other room. He couldn't understand what his colleague was saying, but he heard the voice again.

"You bastard, are you talking law? If I am convinced that you have done the crime, you will spend the rest of your life in jail."

The shouting continued.

Nambi Narayanan felt at ease. He was confident that he could convince the interrogator who was shouting at Sasikumaran. But for the Nth time, he asked the question to himself. *Why did Sasi implicate me?*

▼

8.30 p.m.

Nambi Narayanan was taken to a nearby room, a big one with a large table and bundles of papers on it. At its centre sat the interrogator with blue eyes and chiselled nose. Close to him was a lean, fair man with a thick moustache. The interrogator introduced himself, "M.L. Sharma, IG."

The other man was P.M. Nair, DIG.

"Somehow I felt that you would tell the truth. That is why I kept your interrogation for last. Now, Dr Nambi Narayanan, tell us, what exactly has happened?" M.L. Sharma began his interrogation on a cordial note.

"Sir, I am not a Ph.D. holder. I wanted to do my research at NASA. They had even offered me the facilities. But Dr Sarabhai wanted me to return to India."

Nambi Narayanan divided his presentation into three parts – just like he presented his project reports. The first part was about his family and family background. The second was about his career and career background. And the third was on rocketry and the transfer of rocket technology.

He also said that he had been planning to quit ISRO for a long time.

"But why?"

"Dr A.E. Muthunayagam, Senior to Dr K. Kasturirangan, was to become the Chairman, ISRO. He had given me the impression that he would resign if he was not made the Chairman. In either case, my promotion as Director, LPSC, would have been natural. But he didn't become the Chairman. He didn't resign too. Career-wise, I felt I had reached a dead end. Also, my financial condition is not good. It never was. One more increment may bring me an additional three hundred rupees or so. A couple of my close friends were planning to quit ISRO for similar reasons and to start a fruit farm in Thirunelvelli with an estimated investment of five lakh rupees. I wanted to resign for good."

The clock ticked one. The presentation continued in good flow. Nambi couldn't believe that he could talk so long.

"Take rest. You need to wake up only when you feel like it. We shall question you afterwards," M.L. Sharma rose from his seat and walked briskly to his room, leaving behind the sound of his footsteps.

The next day, it was another Sharma. P.C. Sharma.

"I had been to your house. We searched it. Mr Nambi Narayanan, you don't have a fridge?" he began.

"I had one. I sold it sometime back."

"You could have bought a new one."

"I didn't feel the need. Also, I had other priorities."

"Like what?"

"My sister's daughter's marriage...."

"Why should you spend?"

He explained that his elder sister was depending on him for many things. P.C. Sharma asked a couple of more questions. Then it was the turn of one Ashok Kumar. Then another, and another...

until around 3 p.m., when Pallipuram camp sprang into action. Everybody seemed busy.

CBI Director K. Vijaya Rama Rao was coming.

Nambi Narayanan was taken to another room where he met Vijaya Rama Rao. The Director was sitting majestically flanked by his deputies. Rao interrogated Nambi Narayanan for more than two hours.

Same questions. Same answers.

"Okay," Rao said. "But, do you think Sasikumaran had sold something?"

His very name made Nambi Narayanan sick. But he didn't hesitate to say no.

"It is just not possible to do any espionage in this area. It took seventeen years for ISRO to launch PSLV after we bought the technology of Viking from France."

Then he went one step ahead.

"Even if someone can get some drawings, no idiot would buy them for a price. If such an idiot exists, we can also sell our sand as gold to him."

He then told the CBI top brass about ISRO's failed attempt to illegally transfer cryogenic rocket technology from Glavkosmos through Url Aviation after Air India had declined to carry the cargoes for want of documents.

The CBI Director looked straight into the eyes of Nambi Narayanan for a few seconds. He then leaned forward, took both hands of Nambi Narayanan in his hands, and said, "We are fairly clear that no espionage has taken place. We may take some more time to complete the formalities. I am sorry for what has happened to you. I feel ashamed. It is a sin. But, please try to take it easy..."

It was the climax. Or the anti-climax.

Nambi Narayanan shivered from inside. He couldn't control his feelings. He cried aloud to his heart's content. The first cry since he was arrested.

There was absolute silence in the room but for the shrill cry that rocked the room. After two or three minutes, he felt a pat on his shoulders.

"Cool down. Justice will be done to you," Vijaya Rama Rao said.

Nambi Narayanan was allowed to return to his room. Nobody escorted him. His handcuffs were removed. He fell on his bed and slept.

Sometime in the night, he woke up and wondered why Siby Mathews, the SIT leader, didn't want to listen to him, though he had requested the DIG for a patient listening. He was confident he could convince the police officer that he and his friends in ISRO were doing something beneficial to ISRO, under instructions from the Chairman, though they all knew the operation was illegal and risky.

'Had Siby Mathews listened to me as the CBI top brass has done,' Nambi Narayanan soliloquized, 'the case would have been dropped and I need not have to be in the hell I am in.'

It is this utter callousness on the part of Siby Mathews that sowed in Nambi Narayanan the first seeds of grouse against him, which only intensified day after day, though he has no complaint that Siby Mathews had tortured him or misbehaved with him.

But, if Siby Mathews had given him more than those "one-and-a-half minutes..."

▼

17 December 1994.

CBI office, Malligai, Chennai

All the accused were paraded one by one to identify Raman Srivastava.

M.L. Sharma and his deputies came to know the shocking fact that none of the accused had seen Srivastava before.

It was here that Mariam Rasheeda said that Inspector Vijayan had shown her the photographs of Raman Srivastava, both in uniform and mufti, for 'identifying' him as Brigadier Srivastava.

It was here, after ten days of interrogation, the super cop D.R. Karthikeyan, who later became the Director of CBI, and Arun Bhagat, who later became Director IB, interrogated the accused and realized with a rude shock that the ISRO espionage case was a baseless one fabricated by IB and Kerala Police.

And then, Nambi Narayanan, like every other accused, had his encounter with the polygraph machine.

Dr Lehari from the Central Forensic Laboratory, in his early sixties, was a man who believed machines would never lie, unlike men. So he was surprised when Nambi Narayanan told him that he would like to test the machine.

"Why not!" the old man suddenly turned very friendly.

"But how are you going to test my purer than god machine?" he asked.

"Give me a sheet of paper and a pen," Nambi Narayanan said.

He cut the paper into six pieces of equal size. On the four pieces, he wrote one name each – that of his wife, son, granddaughter and father. On the remaining two pieces, he wrote the same name, Geetha - his daughter. He kept one from the two with him and gave the rest five pieces to Dr Lehari.

The instrument used to conduct polygraph tests consisted of a physiological recorder that assesses three indicators of autonomic arousal using computerized recording systems – heart rate/ blood pressure, respiration and skin conductivity.

Nambi Narayanan's body was connected to the machine. The machine measured his blood pressure, heartbeat, pulse, etc.

"The paper you hold has the name of your wife written on it," Dr Lehari began the test.

"No," Nambi Narayanan answered.

Dr Lehari repeated the same question, changing the names. And he repeated 'No' to all the five questions. It meant he told four truths and one lie. Nambi asked Dr Lehari to tell him which of his questions had he lied to and what was the name on the paper in his hand at that time.

"Geetha," Dr Lehari replied.

He showed Nambi Narayanan the graph corresponding to each of his questions. The one corresponding to the lie had greater amplitude. The technocrat was amazed. He tested the machine once again for validity. Once again, the lie was detected.

And, then the real test began.

▼

Are you Nambi Narayanan?

Yes.

Are you working in ISRO?

Yes.

Have you met Mariam Rasheeda before?

No.

Did you receive money from Fauziya?

No.

Do you know Sasikumaran?

Yes.

Do you know he is a spy?

No.

Do you know Raman Srivastava?

No.

Do you know he is an IG?

Yes.

Have you ever stolen anything from your home?

Yes.

Have you stolen anything from your office?

No.

Do you think Sasikumaran has done espionage?

No.

Have you met Zuheira?

No.

Have you been to Madras International?

No.

Have you been to Hotel Fort Manor?

Yes.

The session went on for six-and-a-half hours. Then, both the men and the machine looked tired.

Dr Lehari was choked with emotion. "We have done a sin," he said repeatedly. He got the signature of S. Nambi Narayanan on all the graphs and countersigned.

"Truth will triumph," he said before Nambi Narayanan, tired yet relaxed, walked towards his room. As he was walking, he remembered the verse he saw on the wall of D.R. Karthikeyan's room.

Pray to God. He will come. He will not come quickly.
But be assured that HE WILL COME.

15

Lie and Truth: Face to Face

30 April 1996

After eighteen months of investigation, R.S. Dhankar, Dy. SP, CBI, submitted the Closure Report in the court of the CJM, Ernakulam[54].

The 104-page report, spread over 115 paragraphs, ruptured the spy ring theory with meticulous precision. It is interesting to juxtapose the IB-Kerala Police theory and the CBI findings – seating lie and truth face-to-face.

THE LIE

K. Chandrasekhar, S.K. Sharma, D. Sasikumaran and Raman Srivastava met Fauziya Hassan and Zuheira at Hotel International, Madras, and handed over the flight data of PSLV in exchange for one lakh American dollars which Mohiyuddin of Habib Bank, Maldives, had given to Fauziya on 19 January 1994.

Chandrasekhar, Sasikumaran and Raman Srivastava had a separate round of discussion about the prospects of setting up a factory of bulletproof vests, using carbon technology developed by Sasikumaran. The meetings were held on 24 January 1994, at Hotel International, Madras.

---

54. Under section 173 (2) CrPC to close the case, R.C 11(S) 94, as "false and baseless"

THE TRUTH

- No person by the name of Mohiyuddin had worked in Habib Bank in the past five years or so.
- Zuheira had not visited India since June 1993.
- As per the records of LPSC, Valiamala, D. Sasikumaran Dy. Director, Cryogenic Unit, had come to the office on 24 January 1994, but had not used his office vehicle. Further investigation revealed that he had gone to Kollamn for the funeral of his daughter's mother-in-law. Authorities of Upasana Hospital, Kollam, confirmed the death. Any number of witnesses testified the presence of Sasikumaran with his wife at the funeral.
- As per his tour note and logbook of the car KL 02-A/ 9100, Raman Srivastava IG (South Zone) was in Thiruvananthapuram in connection with the Republic Day parade. V.R. Rajeevan, City Police Commissioner, and Maj S. Suresh Kumar, Commander of the Republic Day Parade, confirmed the presence of Srivastava in Thiruvananthapuram on 24 January 1994.
- As per the wireless logbook, Raman Srivastava had established contact with his subordinates over wireless during 22-24 January 1994.
- Srivastava's foster father Dr R.C. Srivastava had a head injury on 22 January 1994 and was admitted to Cosmopolitan Hospital, Thiruvananthapuram. Dr Srivastava died on 7 February. Hospital authorities confirmed the visit of Raman Srivastava daily to the hospital.
- S. Nambi Narayanan, Project Director of the Cryogenic Unit didn't attend office on 23 January 1994. One of his colleagues had passed away that day and Nambi Narayanan, along with many employees of the ISRO, was at his house. More than 300 persons, including ISRO staff, vouched for his presence at the funeral that evening. The next day he attended office. A couple

of purchase orders signed on that day testify to his presence in the office. On 25 January, he celebrated the first birthday of his granddaughter. Nearly a hundred persons, relatives and office friends attended the function.

- The records of Hotel International, Madras show no bookings of any room in the name of any of the accused.
- Front Office Manager and Bell Captain of the hotel on duty on 24 January 1994 couldn't identify photographs of any of the 'spies'.

THE LIE

On 25 June 1994, S.K. Sharma, as instructed by K. Chandrasekhar, took Mariam Rasheeda and Fauziya Hassan to Rajinder Singh Institute, Bangalore, better known as Army Club, where they were introduced to Raman Srivastava. He was introduced to them as Brigadier Srivastava.

Fauziya Hassan handed over to him $ 25,000, which Mariam Rasheeda had brought. It actually came through Fauziya's daughter Nasiha from the same Mohiyuddin of Habib Bank, Maldives.

THE TRUTH

- On 25 June, S.K. Sharma got a phone call from his friend K. Chandrasekhar in the morning. Sharma and his business partner Ramasrey went to Chandrasekhar's house where they were introduced to Mariam Rasheeda and Fauziya Hassan. Chandrasekhar wanted Sharma's help for the admission of Fauziya's daughter, Zila Hamdi, in Baldwin Girl's High School through his friend Thomas.
- In the evening, when Sharma was getting ready to go to the school, where he had asked the Maldivians to wait for him, Squadron Leader K.L. Bhasin, his father-in-law's friend, and wife came to his house. Bhasin accompanied Sharma to the school.

- After the admission issue was settled, Sharma drove the Maldivians back to Cooks Town. On the way, they went to the Army Club because Fauziya wanted to go to the toilet. Bhasin offered the Maldivians soft drinks. Sharma and Bhasin took some beverages. Records of the Club confirm the visit.
- Wireless records of the Kerala Police show the presence of Raman Srivastava in Thiruvananthapuram from 23-26 June 1994. He had contacted Deputy Commissioner of Police, Thiruvananthapuram, three times on 23; contacted S.I. Cantonment once; and Deputy Commissioner four times on 24 June. He had talked to V.R. Rajeevan, Police Commissioner, five times on 24 June, and once on 26 June.
- Again, if the IG had gone out of station during this period, the Police Commissioner said, he would have known it.
- The car log book of Raman Srivastava also testifies to Srivastava's presence in Thiruvananthapuram at that time.

THE LIE

On 23 September 1994, D. Sasikumaran, S. Nambi Narayanan, K. Chandrasekhar and S.K. Sharma met Mohammed Aslam, Abdul Haleel, and Zuheira in Room No 108, Hotel Lucia, Thiruvananthapuram. Nambi Narayanan had with him four bundles of complete drawings of PSLV. The deal was struck for nine lakh US dollars. Pakistan was the buyer. Raman Srivastava took the bag containing the cash.

THE TRUTH

- No person by the name Zuheira had stayed in Hotel Lucia during 20-25 September 1994.
- One G.S. Naikwadi, Foreman, Air India was staying in Room No. 108 from 23 to 30 September 1994.

- Nambi Narayanan and Sasikumaran had attended office at 9 a.m. on 23 September. Both went to LPSC in the morning in the company of ISRO scientists P. Mohana Prasad, Dr K. Ramamurthy, and V. Gnana Gandhi, by office car No KBU-6863. After 5 p.m. they all returned in the same car.
- S.K. Sharma's presence at East Cultural Association (ECA) Club, Bangalore, on 22 and 23 September 1994 had been confirmed by witnesses.

THE LIE

S. Nambi Narayanan and some other scientists of ISRO, in collusion with P. Ravindra Reddy, Managing Partner of Machine Tools Aid and Reconditioning (MTAR), Hyderabad, had sold the cryogenic technology.

Ravindra Reddy is a close relative of Bhaskar Reddy, former Chief Minister of Andhra Pradesh. P.V. Prabhakar Rao, son of P.V. Narasimha Rao, the then Prime Minister, is his partner.

THE TRUTH

- Ravindra Reddy had received the contract for fabricating the Vikas engine, not the cryogenic engine, in 1984. He knew Nambi Narayanan and many other technocrats of ISRO. But the contract was awarded to him after a number of discussions with the Contract Negotiation Committee comprising Director, LPSC, Additional Secretary, Department of Space, and other senior officials.
- He knew Bhaskar Reddy, but he didn't have any business tie-up with P.V. Prabhakar Rao.
- India didn't have cryogenic technology in 1994.

THE LIE

ISRO lost volumes of confidential and secret documents.

THE TRUTH

- M.L. Sharma, Joint Director, CBI, wrote a letter to Chairman, ISRO on 12 December 1994, requesting him to appoint a committee for conducting an audit of documents/ drawings and let the CBI know the outcome.
- The Director, LPSC, constituted a committee for verification of documents in cryo and non-cryo areas. The committee submitted two reports.
- The first report found that four out of the 5,767 recorded documents in the cryo area were missing. In the non-cryo area also, 529 out of 33,436 documents could not be traced.
- The second report, submitted 44 days later, said the four missing documents in the cryo area were later re-traced.
- In the non-cryo area, after checking and re-checking, 275 out of the 529 documents recorded lost in the first report were retraced. That was less than one per cent of the documents ISRO had. The missing documents were random in nature and do not pertain to a particular system or sub-system.
- The committee then made a significant observation. "As our development is based on in-house drawings and as all the in-house drawings are available, the committee does not see any impact of some small numbers of drawings missing on our programme."
- ISRO doesn't have a system of making documents as top secret, secret, confidential or classified. Since it is a research organisation, any scientist wanting to study any document is free to go to the documentation cell.
- All the 16,800 sheets of drawings issued to the Fabrication Division, where D. Sasikumaran was working, were found intact after he was transferred to Ahmedabad.

16

CBI and the Art of Alibi

It is no secret that the CBI sleuths tortured the accused even harsher than the IB men. All the accused told me in separate interviews for the purpose of writing this book that the CBI interrogators were not different from the IB interrogators as far as torture was concerned.

However, the attitude of CBI underwent a sea change after Nambi Narayanan told CBI Director Vijay Rama Rao about the failed attempt to reverse espionage the cryogenic rocket technology from Glavkosmos to ISRO using Url Aviation and KELTEC.

CBI got the veracity of Nambi Narayanan's statement confirmed through highly-placed sources in Delhi. Once they were convinced that the espionage, if at all it could be termed so, was not from ISRO but to ISRO from Glavkosmos, that too with the whole-hearted support of the top brass in both ISRO and Glavkosmos, CBI took the crucial decision to disprove the alleged 'crime'.

After ISRO had convinced the CBI officers that ISRO didn't have cryogenic rocket technology in 1994, cryogenic missile technology was a technological stupidity, and selling document and drawings of Vikas engine to a leading figure in Glavkosmos was nothing more than a fairy tale meant of kindergarten children, CBI could have closed the case with the simple conclusion that the crime did not exist.

Instead, the whole effort of CBI was to disprove the espionage story of IB and Kerala Police using alibi; to prove that the accused persons were not at the places and on the specific dates mentioned in the crime and they were, as per official records and statements of witnesses, elsewhere, and hence the espionage activities could not have happened.

While alibi is to be raised during the trial by the accused, in the ISRO spy case, one investigation agency (CBI) used alibi to disprove the findings of another investigating agency (Kerala Police). At the same time, CBI didn't address the illegal operations on the part of ISRO and its technocrats viz-a-viz the reverse espionage to bring cryogenic technology to India, clandestinely.

In its closure report submitted before the CJM, Ernakulam, on 30 April 1996, CBI confirmed that Url Aviation was carrying cargo to India, and not the other way round. But CBI didn't ask these pertinent questions:

- What materials were transported from Glavkosmos to ISRO through Url Aviation?
- Whether they were legal?
- If legal, why did Air India object to take the cargo?
- If the cargoes were part of a legally valid transportation, why couldn't ISRO acquire proper documents for transporting them to India?
- What action did ISRO take against Air India for refusing to take the cargo, if ISRO had the necessary documents?
- Was it because they were doing a clandestine and illegal operation that ISRO engaged Url Aviation to carry the cargo after Air India had backed out for want of proper documents?
- Didn't ISRO know it was violating international and Indian trade laws?

- Was the act done with the knowledge of the Department of Space and the Space Commission?
- If the transportation from Glavkosmos was legal, why the materials had to be transported by road to Tashkent in Uzbekistan, and not from any of the five airports in Moscow, for airlifting to India?
- Why didn't the fourth flight of Url Aviation turn up?
- What was the negative link between the fourth flight (if the transportation was legal) and the ISRO spy scandal?
- Did ISRO sue Url Aviation for not transporting the fourth cargo?
- What more items were thus left at Glavkosmos?
- Why didn't ISRO seek compensation from Glavkosmos and Url Aviation for their failure to honour the contract fully, if the transportation was legal?
- Why did the SIT of Kerala Police arrest and torture K. Chandrasekhar, the authorized representative of Glavkosmos?
- Why did Glavkosmos and ISRO proceed with the process of transferring cryogenic technology using KELTEC as a conduit, even after the first agreement containing the technology clause was scrapped, and the second agreement had no technology transfer clause in it?
- If Glavkosmos had chosen KELTEC only to fabricate the cryogenic engine as job work, why should the Managing Director of KELTEC write to the Chairman, Glavkosmos, to send copies of his letter(s) to ISRO Chairman and the Director of Cryogenic System in ISRO?
- If there was nothing clandestine or illegal in the proposed Rs 1,000 million joint venture between KELTEC and Glavkosmos for the manufacture of cryo engine, why was that move aborted in the wake of the espionage case?

- Even if the absurd espionage theory is presumed to be true, what was the alleged role of KELTEC in it?
- Why was K. Sudhakar, MD of KELTEC, interrogated by IB?

It is naïve to conclude that these questions were out of the scope of investigation. The fact is that CBI was fully aware of the illegal and clandestine operations of ISRO that paved the way for the ISRO espionage case. But CBI chose not to open the can of worms.

Maybe CBI wants to pull wool over the clandestine operations of ISRO and its technocrats – an act that led to the espionage case causing unimaginable loss to ISRO, the prime victim of the espionage case.

17

The Crimes of IB

CBI investigation disclosed that even before the arrest of accused Mariam Rasheeda on 20 October 1994, Kerala Police had requested the IB officials for assistance in questioning the accused Mariam Rasheeda. And, in fact, certain IB officials had interrogated Mariam Rasheeda from 16 October onwards.

After the police custody of accused Mariam Rasheeda was obtained, Mathew John, Joint Director, SIB, deputed R.B. Sreekumar, DD, SIB; C.R.R. Nair, Asst. Director; G.S. Nair, DCIO; K. V. Thomas, DCIO, M.J. Punnen, DCIO, and others for interrogation.

P.S. Jaiprakash, ACID-I, Cochin; C.M. Ravindran, Dy. Director, SIB, Mumbai; and V.K. Maini, DCIO, IB Headquarters, Delhi, and others were also deputed for interrogation of the accused.

The CJM gave custody of Mariam Rasheeda to Inspector Vijayan on 3 November 1994. But Vijayan in his Case Diary recorded that IB officials asked him to go out of the room and was kept out of the picture.

Sub-Inspector Ammini Kutty Amma, who was on duty to guard Mariam Rasheeda stated that Mariam was not allowed to sleep during interrogation which continued round the clock for about a week when she was kept standing.[55]

Based on the notes taken by the interrogators, the interrogation reports were compiled. Four such reports in respect of accused Mariam Rasheeda, Fauziya Hassan, D. Sasikumaran and K. Chandrasekhar were made available to CBI by IB when the case was taken over by CBI. After CBI took over the investigation, the six accused were taken into police custody, remand and questioned in detail, mostly based on the information provided by Kerala Police and IB.

The accused completely denied their involvement in any espionage activities and stated they were innocent. When they were confronted with their statements, they stated the statements were made under duress on suggested lines.

The Director IB issued several UO notes to the Cabinet Secretary, Home Minister, Principal Secretary to Prime Minister, Home Secretary and other high functionaries of the Government of India in this regard.

The DIB mentioned the allegation that MTAR Ravindra Reddy was closely related to the Chief Minister, Andhra Pradesh, and had business dealings with Prabhakar Rao (son of the former Prime Minister of India), needed to be verified discreetly.

In his UO note[56] the DIB mentioned that the DGP, Kerala, has to be advised immediately to bring Raman Srivastava, IG of Police, in the ambit of the case and that "sanction of the Government will

---

55. This needs to be viewed in the context of what the Supreme Court of India held in 1984 that "the questioning, by exercise of the power conferred by section 8 of the IOS Act, 1923 must be during the daytime and in no case after sunset and before sunrise."
56. No. 9/ESP (U)/94 (3)-11-309 dated 28 November 1995

be required to take Srivastava into custody as he is a member of the Indian Police Service."

In a subsequent UO note dated 1 December 1994, the DIB mentioned that Srivastava had emerged as the most important member of the inner group of the spy ring. However, neither in this UO note, nor in the subsequent notes, did the DIB spell out the evidence available on record against Srivastava. It is evident from the UO note[57]. The DIB observes "Raman Srivastava, IGP, Thiruvananthapuram, is being examined and his movements etc. are being checked up."

In other words, twenty-one days after the DIB had concluded that Raman Srivastava was an important member of the inner group of the spy ring, IB was still examining his movements!

As regards the role of MTAR Ravindra Reddy, DIB in the aforesaid note further went on to say that "the allegation that one MTAR Ravindra Reddy, a scientist of ISRO was closely related to the CM of Andhra Pradesh, and that he has business dealings with Prabhakar Rao has not been substantiated. Prima facie, there is nothing against Ravindra Reddy in this case."

It is crystal clear that DIB first issued UO notes to the highest functionaries in the Government of India indicating involvement of Raman Srivastava, MTAR Ravindra Reddy[58], and others, and subsequently negated his own version[59].

The investigation further disclosed that Prabhakar Rao S/o Narasimha Rao, Prime Minister of India, had no business dealings with Ravindra Reddy. Reddy was examined in this regard and he denied having any business dealings with Prabhakar Rao.

---

57. No. 334/DIB/DESP/94 dated 22 December 1994
58. P. Ravindra Reddy, Managing Partner of a firm named MTAR
59. Given in the earlier notes

In the course of the investigation, CBI recorded the statements of many police officers who had handled the matter, including Inspector Vijayan, who stated that after IB came into the scene, the IB officials physically took over Rasheeda from the Kerala Police and kept her separately in the CRPF guest house and took charge of the interrogation. He has further stated that on 4 November 1994, the IB officials wanted the local police to be kept out of all the activities, including interrogation, and he was also asked to go out of the room. He has recorded this in the Case Diary dated 4 November 1994.

Ammini Kutty, SI, stated that she was on security duty of Rasheeda, and that after few days of interrogation, the IB officials told Rasheeda in Ammini's presence, that if Rasheeda did not tell the truth, she would be stripped naked and would be made to lie on ice and insects would be thrown on her body. She further stated that the IB officials gave Raman Srivastava's photograph to Rasheeda and asked her to see the photograph for half an hour. Thereafter, they brought another four photographs and kept Srivastava's photograph along with them and asked Mariam Rasheeda to identify the photograph, which she did as suggested. This is a questionable, illegal and unprofessional method adopted by the IB officials to get Srivastava's photograph identified.

G. Babu Raj, SP, CID – who was a part of the investigating team of Kerala Police headed by Siby Mathews – was examined who, inter alia, stated that the IB officials did not share the result of their interrogation of the accused persons with him.

Importantly, he stated that IB had already concluded the involvement of Srivastava in the espionage case even before the case was registered, and therefore, he did not feel it necessary to verify the facts. He has also said, "it was difficult on our part to digest the above conclusion of IB, but we were helpless."

Babu Raj stated about the visit to Bangalore from where he collected the photograph of Sqn. Ldr. K.L. Bhasin. He showed the photograph to Fauziya Hassan at Thiruvananthapuram, which she readily identified as that of the person whom she had seen at Army Club, Bangalore. Babu Raj further stated that he was fully convinced that the person whom Fauziya had met at Bangalore along with Sharma was none other than Sqn. Ldr. K.L. Bhasin.

Siby Mathews vide his letter dated 16 December 1994, addressed to DGP, Kerala, inter alia stated that:

> *...regarding the allegations raised against Raman Srivastava, IG, it is true that the Special Investigation Team has not investigated in that direction. During the discussion with officers of IB at the office of DGP (Intelligence) and also with your good self, I have mentioned that without some incriminating evidence, it is highly embarrassing to enquire about the alleged role of IGP. The officers of IB have not disclosed the grounds for the allegations against IGP. However, I had requested for transferring the case to CBI even earlier through my written communication dated 30 November 1994.*

In this letter, Siby Mathews has further mentioned that the investigating team could not have been a source of leakage to the Press in as much as the diary of Mariam Rasheeda got translated from her native language to English by IB, and this translation was not available with him when the contents of the diary were leaked out to the Press.

During the course of the investigation, the statement of Mathew John, JD, SIB, Thiruvananthapuram, was recorded. He stated that at the request of the Kerala Police, IB got involved in Rasheeda's interrogation. He, however, could not recollect the names of all the IB officers who were detailed for assistance in the interrogation.

After going through the interrogation reports, Mathew John used to communicate the essence of important disclosures to his senior officers. He stated that the involvement of Raman Srivastava was highlighted by the media, but he did not take steps to verify the disclosures of the accused persons, nor questioned Raman Srivastava in this regard.

R.B. Sreekumar, DD, SIB, Thiruvananthapuram, stated that IB offered to assist Kerala Police in the interrogation of the foreign nationals at the request of the former. In his statement, he has admitted that the IB "does not have the legal authority to examine the accused when they are in the custody of the police authority."

During the investigation, the following acts of commission and omission on the part of the IB officers had come to notice of CBI.[60]

- Immediately after the police custody of accused Mariam Rasheeda was obtained on 3 November 1994, IB officials physically took over the accused from the lawful custody of the Kerala Police and disassociated Inspector Vijayan from further interrogation of accused Mariam Rasheeda.
- Similarly, IB officials took over the custody of the other accused persons who were subsequently arrested by Kerala Police and interrogated them, but did not apprise the Kerala Police officers about the revelations allegedly made by the accused persons. Thus, the IB officers conducted the interrogation in a hush-hush manner, dissociating the Kerala Police, for reasons best known to them.
- During interrogation, IB officials tortured at least three accused persons – Mariam Rasheeda, Chandrasekhar and Nambi

60. Letter No. 2782/3/11(S) 94—SIU V/SIC, dated 3 June 1996, addressed to the Secretary, Ministry of Home Affairs, Government of India.

Narayanan. The fact of the ill-treatment of Mariam Rasheeda is proved from the statement of Inspector Vijayan and Ammini Kutty, SI.

- Chandrasekhar and Nambi Narayanan were given medical treatment on 28 November 1994 and 3 December 1994, respectively, which is indicative of the torture meted out to them.
- IB officers interrogated Nambi Narayanan as well as S.K. Sharma, but did not prepare the respective interrogation reports. It appears that their statements were not recorded as they did not toe the line suggested by the IB officials.
- The reports in respect of four accused persons – Fauziya Hassan, Mariam Rasheeda, Chandrasekhar and Sasikumaran – are not dated and are unsigned, due to which it has not been possible to fix up the identity of the particular IB officers who prepared the interrogation reports. As a result, it could not be ascertained on what basis such interrogation reports were prepared.
- The interrogations of accused Fauziya Hassan, Chandrasekhar and Sasikumaran were video recorded by IB officers and the tapes were produced in the Kerala High Court. But none of the IB officers during their examination admitted to having video-graphed the interrogation of the aforesaid accused. Nor did they reveal the name of the IB officer(s) who recorded the interrogations.
- What is surprising is that even the Joint Director, IB, who was overall in-charge of interrogations, failed to identify such officers. The Deputy Director of IB stated he was unaware of the videography.
- The IB officers did not conduct verification about the veracity of the statements of the accused persons for reasons best

known to them. If they had done as properly as any specialised agency would do, the air would have been cleared a long time ago and the honour of respectable scientists could have been saved.

- In the interrogation report of D. Sasikumaran and K. Chandrasekhar, IB has given details of various meetings in which, besides the accused, Raman Srivastava had also participated. But IB did not share with Kerala Police the basis of allegations against Raman Srivastava, as is evident from the letter dated 16 December 1994 of Siby Mathews, addressed to DGP, Kerala.
- Mathew John, Joint Director, IB, had sent a message dated 25 November 1994 to Director, IB, stating therein that the disclosures made by the accused persons were a mixture of truths, half-truths and untruths. It is thus clear that even the senior officer of IB suspected that the revelations made by the accused were not worthy of credence.
- Notwithstanding this, the IB officials did not conduct verification of the disclosures allegedly made by the accused. If they had made the verifications at that time, arrests of innocent persons could have been avoided.
- The interrogation reports as recorded by IB officers are incoherent and full of contradictions and do not give the exact nature of documents that were allegedly passed on to foreign agents. Rather, they have blandly recorded that the drawings/documents of the Viking engine and the Cryogenic engine were secreted out. Further, they failed to reconcile the statements as the statements contradicted each other on several points.
- The above-mentioned facts show that the aforesaid IB officials comprising the team enquiring into the ISRO case acted in an unprofessional manner and were privy to the arrest of six

innocent persons, thereby causing them immense mental and physical agony. The senior officers who were supervising and monitoring the enquiries under reference, particularly, Mathew John, Jt. Director, and R.B. Sreekumar, failed in their duty to conduct the inquiry in an objective and fair manner.

- At the IB headquarter, the UO notes referred to herein were prepared based on these interrogation reports and without verification, leading to serious complications including casting doubts on the integrity of two top ISRO scientists who were responsible for developing the PSLV project and launching our country into space.

18

The Wrongs of Kerala Police

In its letter to the Government of Kerala, CBI listed out certain acts of omission and commission on the part of following Kerala Police officers when the investigation was in their hands.[61]

1. Inspector Vijayan

- S. Vijayan, Inspector, Special Branch, questioned Mariam Rasheeda and Fauziya Hassan when the Maldivian women approached him for getting the necessary permission for Mariam Rasheeda to stay beyond 90 days permitted by her visa. He advised Mariam Rasheeda to get a confirmed ticket for her return. Accordingly, she purchased an Indian Airlines ticket: Thiruvananthapuram to Male (W/L), and another of Sri Lankan Airlines: Thiruvananthapuram to Colombo; both for 17 October 1994.
- Vijayan, however, kept the tickets of Mariam Rasheeda with him unauthorizedly, and on 20 October 1994, arrested her at 4:15 p.m. and lodged a complaint with Vanchiyoor Police Station. The seizure of the tickets was not shown even after the registration of the case and thus, he obstructed Mariam Rasheeda's return to the Maldives on 17 October 1994.

61. Letter No. 2783/3/11(S) 94—SIU V/SIC, dated 3 June 1996, addressed to the Chief Secretary, Government of Kerala.

- He took over the investigation of Crime No. 225/94 on 3 November 1994 and he was entrusted with police custody of Mariam Rasheeda from 3 to 14 November 1994 by the CJM, Thiruvananthapuram. But he willfully surrendered the custody of accused Mariam Rasheeda to the IB officials in contravention of the Court orders and caused the IB officials alone interrogating Mariam Rasheeda and torturing her. Vijayan recorded in his several Case Diaries that the IB officials had asked him to get out of the room and therefore he had to leave the room, leaving the accused lady to the male officials of IB. He is, thus, liable for dereliction and abrogation of legal duties.
- On 9 November 1994, Mariam Rasheeda disclosed about her contacts with the accused, Sasikumaran and Chandrasekhar. But Vijayan took no steps to question either D. Sasikumaran or K. Chandrasekhar and to confront them with Mariam Rasheeda to bring out the truth, especially in the context of wide media coverage from 21 October 1994 onwards, alleging espionage activities.
- The basis of his deduction that Mariam Rasheeda and Fauziya Hassan had come to India for espionage purposes have not been brought out on record by him. During the investigation, he did not collect any information about any particular espionage activity committed by the accused.
- Though till 12 November 1994, no evidence had come on record about any espionage activities, he lodged a report with Vanchiyoor Police Station on 13 November 1994 that Rasheeda and Fauziya, in collusion with certain Indians and foreign nationals, had taken part in activities against the sovereignty and integrity of India and indulged in activities prejudicial to the cordial relations India had with its neighbours.

- Even though he did not mention any specific activity committed by the accused, Crime No 246/94 (espionage case) under the Official Secrets Act, 1923 was registered and six accused persons were arrested.
- The main grounds mentioned in the FIR for an allegation of espionage is that Mariam Rasheeda contacted D. Sasikumaran several times and that she had made a lot of entries in her diary which was seized by the police. Verification of these telephone calls and a translation of the diary entries would have confirmed that they had nothing to do with ISRO or espionage. Without any verification, he asked in haste to lodge an FIR on allegations of espionage. He, thus, acted in an unfair and unprofessional manner, thereby causing avoidable harassment and sufferings to the accused persons.
- While the accused Mariam Rasheeda was in his custody, he allowed the IB officials to ill-treat her. He had also threatened her of dire consequences.
- In his statement, he had admitted having shown a photograph of Raman Srivastava to Mariam Rasheeda. But strangely enough, he did not bring this fact on record. Nor did he bring on record the rationale of why only Raman Srivastava's photograph was shown to Rasheeda. This shows mala fide intent and a lack of professional integrity on his part.

2. K.K. Joshua

- K.K. Joshua, the then DSP, CH, CID, Thiruvananthapuram was drafted in the SIT which took over the investigation of the case on 15 November 1994. He was assigned the job of preparing the case records.
- In his Case Diary dated 16 November 1994, he recorded that both Fauziya Hassan and Mariam Rasheeda admitted that they

had come to India to collect vital information for some agents of alien countries and that they contacted D. Sasikumaran, a scientist of LPSC, K. Chandrasekhar of Bangalore, and others and collected valuable information and passed the same to foreign countries. However, he did not record the statements of the accused on 16 November 1994. Neither did he mention the details of the alleged valuable information.

- Assuming that it became known to him on 16 November 1994 that valuable information had been passed on to foreign countries, he took no immediate steps to recover any incriminating documents by way of conducting the house searches of D. Sasikumaran and K. Chandrasekhar. It may be mentioned that their names had figured even during the investigation of Crime No. 225/94.
- It is on record that the interrogations of Fauziya Hassan, K. Chandrasekhar and D. Sasikumaran were video-graphed by IB, but the same has not been indicated in the Case Records, in spite of the fact that the custody of the accused was with the Kerala Police.
- Though it has been brought on record that the accused were interrogated by IB officials, no interrogation report, whatsoever, prepared by IB was taken on record by him. Nor did he verify the allegations contained in the statements.
- The statement of accused S.K. Sharma was recorded on 3 December 1994, but the corresponding CD has not been issued by him.
- The accused, during questioning by CBI, have stated that they were mentally and physically tortured during the police custody, as a result of which they had to make statements on suggested lines. The investigation also disclosed that S. Nambi Narayanan and K. Chandrasekhar were given medical treatment while

in police custody on 3 December 1994 and 28 November 1994, respectively. However, he suppressed the fact of medical treatment given to the accused from the Case Diaries and Case Records.

- Accused K. Chandrasekhar in his statement dated 28 November 1994 had allegedly stated that Raman Srivastava IG attended the meeting at International Hotel, Madras, on 22/23 January 1994 and subsequently attended a meeting at Indira Nagar Club, Bangalore, in September 1994. Joshua took no steps either to question Raman Srivastava or check the official records which were available to ascertain his movements.
- On the one hand, Kerala Police was suspecting espionage activities; on the other hand, they delayed the conduct of house searches, etc., to recover incriminating documents, if any. It is clear from the fact that the house and office search of accused D. Sasikumaran at LPSC, Valiamala, were conducted on 30 November 1994 even though he was arrested on 21 November 1994. There is nothing on record to justify such a delayed search. Similarly, though S. Nambi Narayanan was arrested on 30 November 1994, a house search was not conducted till the case was handed over to CBI on 4 December 1994.

3. Siby Mathews

- Siby Mathews, DIG, Crime, was heading the Special Investigation Team and was, therefore, fully responsible for the conduct of investigation in the aforesaid two cases.
- An investigation conducted by CBI has revealed that he did not take adequate steps either concerning the thorough interrogation of the accused persons by Kerala Police or verification of the so-called disclosures made by the accused

persons. He left the entire investigation to IB, surrendering his duties.

- S. Nambi Narayanan got medically checked up while in custody, in the Hindustan Latex Guest House by Dr V. Sukumaran of Sri Krishna Hospital, Trivandrum. The doctor was brought to the guest house by Inspector Vijayan in a blue Maruti car. The doctor found both legs of Nambi Narayanan swollen with multiple haemorrhage rashes. He had also prescribed medicines for him. Similarly, K. Chandrasekhar had to be rushed to the hospital on 28 November 1994, where two sets of ECG were taken.
- The Case Diaries of Kerala Police did not record either of these. However, Siby Mathews, DIG, who was the leader of the SIT, pleaded ignorance of the treatment given to the accused who were remanded under his custody.
- He ordered the indiscriminate arrest of the ISRO scientists and others without adequate evidence on record. It is stressed that neither Siby Mathews nor his team recovered any incriminating ISRO documents from the accused persons or any money alleged to have been paid to the accused persons by their foreign masters. It was unprofessional on his part to have ordered indiscriminate arrests of top ISRO scientists who played a key role in the successful launching of satellites into space, thereby causing avoidable mental and physical agony to them.
- He sent a report vide his letter dated 16 December 1994 to DGP, Kerala, stating therein that it was embarrassing for him to conduct further investigation into the alleged role of Raman Srivastava since the IB officials had not told him the grounds on which they were suspecting Raman Srivastava's involvement. Being a senior officer, he should have verified the facts from all possible angles and conducted investigation professionally and thereafter taken a clear and firm stand on the role of Raman

Srivastava. Unfortunately, he allowed the doubts and suspicions in the media and the public mind to linger on.

- While handing over the Case Records to CBI, Siby Mathews in his CD dated 4 December 1994 recorded that CBI should conduct investigation on certain points, namely, the office and house search of S. Nambi Narayanan; verification of investments made by the accused persons with Thomas Kurisinkal of Cochin; fixing up the identity of Brigadier also known as Coatwala; nature of secret documents alleged to have been secreted out by Mohammed Pasha/ Mohiyuddin, and verification of the records of Hotel Madras International regarding the stay of the accused persons there on 24 January 1994, etc.
- It is important to mention that he took over the charge of the cases on 15 November 1994. The case continued with him till 4 December 1994, for about 20 days. Surprisingly, he did not take any steps at his level to investigate the points suggested by him. Since Siby Mathews was based at Thiruvananthapuram, there was no justification for not having the searches conducted in the official/residential premises of accused S. Nambi Narayanan, though Nambi Narayanan was arrested by the Kerala Police on 30 November 1994.
- Even though accused D. Sasikumaran was arrested on 21 November 1994, his house search was conducted on 30 November i.e., nine days later, for which there is no justification. This shows a lack of professionalism on his part.
- G. Babu Raj, the then SP, CB, CID, Thiruvananthapuram, in his CD dated 24 November 1994, clearly recorded that the person who had accompanied Rasheeda and Fauziya to the Army Club at Bangalore in June '94 was Sqn. Ldr. K.L. Bhasin. He ruled out the possibility of Raman Srivastava's presence in the said Club along with the Maldivian women. The Case Diary is presumed

to have been submitted to Siby Mathews, being in charge of the team.

- It is intriguing that Siby Mathews did not take any steps to educate the media about the outcome of the investigation conducted by his team on this aspect and thus, deliberately and intentionally allowed the rumours to float uninterrupted, resultantly causing deep embarrassment to Raman Srivastava.
- It may be added that notwithstanding the clear findings that were given by his SP, Siby Mathews, before handing over the case to CBI, recorded in his CD dated 4 December 1994 that further investigation was required to be conducted to firmly fix up the identity of Brigadier or Coatwala. It is not known as to why he did not enquire into this aspect himself for 20 days when the case was being supervised by him. It is also not clear why Siby Mathews did not examine Raman Srivastava in this matter. It appears that he deliberately and intentionally allowed the investigation to drift for reasons best known to him.
- Siby Mathews in his statement admitted that a photograph of K.L. Bhasin was collected at Bangalore. On return to Thiruvananthapuram, the photograph of Bhasin was shown to accused Fauziya Hassan who identified the photograph of Bhasin as that of the person with whom she and Mariam Rasheeda went to a place that looked like the Army Club at Bangalore. However, this fact was not brought on record.
- Siby Mathews and his team failed miserably, even in conducting verification of the records of hotels – Hotel Fort Manor, Hotel Pankaj, Hotel Luciya, among others – located at Thiruvananthapuram to ascertain the veracity of the statements of accused persons. Similarly, he failed to get the records of Hotel International, Madras checked up even though the investigation remained with him for close to three weeks.

Part - V

Facts Stranger than Fiction

19

Judicial Trespassing

The ISRO espionage case put to test every institution and agency in India. Barring one or two, the rest failed.

1 April 1998

In the Supreme Court of India, a Division Bench was in session.

Justice M.K. Mukherjee and Justice Syed Shah Mohammad Quadri were hearing the final argument in a cluster of Special Leave Petitions challenging the Kerala High Court's decision not to quash the State government notification for further investigation in the ISRO espionage case. Nearly fifteen months after the SLPs were admitted, the Supreme Court was completing the argument.

Counsels for the accused had completed their argument, exposing the illegality of the government notification and its *mala fide* intentions.

Kerala government was making a last-ditch effort to save its face and salvage the members of the Special Investigation Team from the possibility of being prosecuted for having fabricated a spy scandal.

Shanti Bhushan, former Union Minister for Law and Justice, who was appearing for the Kerala State government, thought the attitude of the Court would undergo a sea change once the judges view video cassettes of confessions of the accused, which the IB officials had recorded. So the counsel pleaded:

"Honourable Judges may be pleased to view the video cassettes containing confessions of the accused to get more clarity regarding the case."

"Who made the video cassettes?" the Bench asked.

"The IB," the counsel replied.

"Under what provision of law does IB have the authority to make video cassettes of interrogation?" the Bench wanted to know.

The former Union Minister for Law and Justice didn't answer. He looked at M.K. Damodaran, Advocate-General of Government of Kerala, who saved Shanti Bhushan from further embarrassment.

"IB only helped in making the video. It was actually the Kerala Police who made them," said M.K. Damodaran.

The Advocate General was telling a lie. The affidavit filed by DGP Kerala before the Supreme Court in the case the court was considering had stated that the video cassettes were made by IB.

The Advocate General was hiding a very important fact from the Supreme Court. A Division Bench of Kerala High Court, in its judgment[62] had put on record that the video cassettes were made by IB.

"Why should we view video cassettes which are not admissible under the law?" the Bench asked, and declined to see the video cassettes.

But, a Division Bench of Kerala High Court had thought differently. It summoned privileged documents from CBI even before the investigation was complete. It viewed and reviewed the video cassettes produced by IB which are not admissible under the law. It ridiculed and grilled CBI for arriving at a conclusion, which was incongruent with the illegal reports of IB. It castigated CBI for

---

62. W.A. No. 1676/94—C (in O.P. No. 17367 of 1994—P) delivered on 13 January 1995

being biased. It directed CBI to act in a more efficient and vigilant manner without any pre-conceived notions, after patting IB on its back for its illegal acts.

The judicial trespassing by two learned senior judges in Kerala High Court was made on 13 January 1995.

Before that, a quick glance back.

Once CBI assumed charge of the investigation, the avalanche of media reports on the supposedly confidential interrogation stopped abruptly. And quite contrary to the media speculations, CBI didn't arrest Raman Srivastava though *The Indian Express,* quoting IB reports, had flashed the arrest as a foregone conclusion.

Ten days after CBI began its investigation, a legal forum in Kochi moved a PIL before Kerala High Court seeking the arrest of Raman Srivastava and his removal from service invoking Article 311 of the Constitution of India.

The court dismissed the PIL since "no court can direct the Investigating agency to implicate one as an accused and arrest him."

An appeal was preferred and the case was posted before a Division Bench.

▼

28 December 1994

COURT NO VII— A Division Bench of Justice K. Sreedharan and Justice B.N. Patnaik was on session.

"Which officer is investigating the case?" the Bench asked.

"R.S. Dhankar, Deputy SP," counsel for CBI answered.

"Have you received any information regarding the role of Raman Srivastava in the case?"

"Investigation is progressing. Six persons have so far been arrested. They have been questioned in detail. Legal steps will be initiated against the accused."

"Six or sixteen, it is none of our concern. What we want is definite information on whether Srivastava has any role in it? Have you received any documentary evidence from CBI? What is your difficulty in divulging the details?"

"Investigation is progressing."

"Has CBI questioned Srivastava?"

"Yes."

The court then directed the Director, CBI, to produce all records relating to the questioning of Raman Srivastava, IG of police.

▼

3 January 1995

The ISRO case was posted number two in the list before the same Bench.

"I am not making any comments on the record," the court began its proceedings, "but the records show the investigation has backtracked since 12 December. What went wrong?"

The CBI counsel kept silent.

Justice K. Sreedharan opened a cover and read the affidavit filed by Surinder Pal, Dy. SP, CBI, submitting that Srivastava has no role in the ISRO espionage case.

"We have verified the entire records produced by CBI. The records have facts that can link Srivastava to the case. We won't let it go like this. How did CBI conclude that Srivastava has no role?" the Bench posed.

"State police tortured the accused to implicate Srivastava in the case."

A visibly annoyed Justice K. Sreedharan raised his voice: "It is a serious allegation against the Kerala Police if you charge they tried to implicate a top rung IPS officer. Did CBI conduct any investigation to find out the veracity of the allegation? Isn't it absolutely necessary that such officers who tried to implicate an IG in a case be sent out from the force?"

The CBI counsel kept silent.

"Who is the chief of CBI, the famous investigating agency?" the court asked.

"K. Vijaya Rama Rao."

"Has he seen the records? Studied them? He has to file a detailed affidavit. How much time do you need?"

"Fifteen days."

"Fifteen days! It is a disgrace to your officers. We can give time till Monday," the court said.

It was a Wednesday. There were only three more working days. Yet, the CBI Director filed his affidavit before the deadline. It stated:

> *A serious doubt has arisen with regard to all the essential facts on the basis of which initial suspicion against him (Raman Srivastava) was created. The oral and documentary evidence collected during the investigation conducted by CBI so far is found to be inconsistent with the allegations contained in the interrogation reports of the accused persons. It may also be mentioned that Raman Srivastava was not identified by any of the concerned persons.*

▼

9 January 1995

This time it was K.T.S. Tulsi, Additional Solicitor General of Government of India, who appeared for CBI. He directly attacked the writ on the *locus standi* of the petitioner.

Court: PIL would stand in cases on the environment and human rights. Why can't this be considered a PIL?

Tulsi: In a criminal case, even the court can interfere only after the final report is submitted before it. The right to investigate rests with the police, and police only. The investigation, in this case, is progressing. And Srivastava is not an accused.

Court: While perusing the records, we felt there is *prima facie* evidence linking Srivastava to the case.

Tulsi: We don't depend on the statements of the accused. Our investigation is independent. Our aim is to convince the court that the investigation is moving on the right track.

▼

13 January 1995

The Bench passed its orders, upholding the decision of the single bench. "No court can direct the Investigating agency to implicate one as an accused and arrest him."

But then, the Kerala High Court trespassed. "The report of Intelligence Bureau which has its own investigating machinery, in unmistakable terms found the involvement of Raman Srivastava in the case."

The observation proved to be more explosive than RDX. Raman Srivastava was suspended. Chief Minister K. Karunakaran had to resign. The credibility of CBI was questioned.

The attitude and order of the court raise many uncomfortable questions.

When the court upheld the decision of the single bench that no court can direct the investigating agency to implicate a person and arrest him during the investigation stage, the court was making it clear that, at that point in time, the court had no legal jurisdiction to enter into the merit of the case.

If so, what compelled the court to trespass and make a ruling about Raman Srivastava's involvement in the spy ring?

How could two senior judges of the High Court put on record a glaring flaw that IB has its own investigating machinery?

Could it be possible the two learned judges were unaware of the fact that IB is an organization with absolutely no right to investigate?

Could it be possible that the senior judges were oblivious of the legal position that a person remanded under police custody should not be interrogated by a person or agency that has no legal authority to interrogate the accused?

Why did the Division Bench view the video cassettes produced by IB which was the result of an illegal act?

Are judges not bound by the rule of law?

Was the Bench ignorant of the fact that videographing the interrogation of a non-convicted arrested person is a blatant violation of the Identification of the Prisoners Act, 1920?

Instead of watching the illegally made out video cassettes containing statements of the accused and making absurd rulings based on them, why didn't the Division Bench pull up IB for doing an illegal act (of interrogating the accused under police custody and producing video cassettes of the forced confessions)?

CBI in its Closure Report submitted before CJM, Ernakulam, on 30 April 1996 brings out an important observation on the statements of the accused, reportedly made by IB officials.

> *Strangely, they (IB officers) didn't remember before whom the accused had made the statements. Some of the officers, when shown the interrogation report of the four accused obtained from its Thiruvananthapuram office, said they were not sure whether the reports did, in fact, originate from the Thiruvananthapuram office."*

If so, was the Division Bench referring to some fictitious report when it observed on 13 January 1995 that the "reports of IB, which had its own investigating machinery, in unmistakable terms found the involvement of Raman Srivastava in the case?"

Is any court in India empowered to deny an Indian citizen his rights under Articles 14 and 21 of the Constitution?

Who is liable for the wrongs committed by the judiciary?

It is an accepted legal position that the State is liable for the wrongs committed by the judicial wing of the State, though the judges are not personally liable because of the provisions of the Judicial Officer's Protection Act.

The State here is not the government, but the State of India consisting of Executive, Legislature and Judiciary as defined under Article 12 of the Constitution of India.

Did the State come to the protection of Raman Srivastava, whose career and life suffered due to the illegal and questionable actions of the said Division Bench of the Kerala High Court?

▼

It is true that the judges don't have an easy job. They repeatedly do what the rest of us seek to avoid – make decisions. It is equally true that the innocent suffers when the judges err.

The victim can prove his innocence and avoid being punished (*de jure*) by getting the wrong decision of the learned judge annulled through an appeal, provided he has money and the mental strength to fight prolonged legal battles.

But what about the *de facto* punishment?

For instance, how is the system going to compensate for the injury caused to Raman Srivastava and his family by the observations of the Division Bench?

How is it going to compensate for the loss K. Karunakaran had to suffer when the observations triggered a political coup in Kerala?

Again, how is it going to compensate for the erosion of trust ordinary people would like to have in the judiciary?

It is interesting to know how the judgment has affected the judges who delivered the wrong judgment. In no way, it seems.

Justice B.N. Patnaik retired delivering justice (he died in June, 2020). Justice K. Sreedharan, who retired as the Chief Justice of Gujarat in 1998, was later appointed the Kerala Lok Ayukta.

It is high time the country does some rethinking on the immunity the protectors of justice enjoy under the Judicial Officer's Protection Act.

Do they need that immunity when even a former Prime Minister can be tried like any other citizen in a criminal court?

Can judicial trespassing be allowed in a civilized society?

And what about the judicial accountability that calls for making the judges responsible for the decision they deliver all by themselves? Every public officer of the state is responsible to the public for the decision she/ he takes.

Sanjib Banerjee, Chief Justice of Madras High Court puts it straight. "Respectability of the judiciary comes from accountability. We need to introspect to see to what extent we are accountable. As being part of society, we reflect both the good and the bad of society. There are rotten apples among us. As long as we are accountable, and we expose these rotten apples, we will have the respectability we deserve." (*The Hindu*, 30 April 2021)

20

Missing the Woods for the Trees

While Kerala Police and CBI were oblivious of the provisions of the Act based on which they were investigating a crime of espionage, one Magistrate thought the wrong he was doing was right and another Magistrate paraded his legal ignorance by 'overruling' the ruling of a Division Bench of the High Court of Kerala. While the Supreme Court missed the woods for the trees, the Marxist leadership 'overruled' even the ruling of the Supreme Court.

On 30 April 1996, CBI filed its Closure Report before the CJM, Ernakulam,[63] concluding the espionage case as "false and baseless". Two days later, the CJM accepted the report and discharged all the accused.

But the law says the CJM should not have acted upon the CBI report of investigation, for two reasons.

Firstly, the Magistrate should not have taken cognizance of the Closure Report filed before it by CBI[64] because Section 173 (2) (i) reads, "As soon as it (investigation) is completed, the officer in charge of the police station shall forward to a Magistrate empowered to take cognizance of the offence on a police report, a report in the form prescribed by the State government."

---

63. Under Section 173(2) of CrPC
64. Under Section 173(2) CrPC

The CJM, Ernakulam was not empowered to take cognizance of the report since he didn't get a complaint in writing from the Central government or "some officer empowered by the central government for this purpose"; something mandatory under Section 13 (3) of the Indian Official Secrets Act, 1923.[65]

Secondly, CBI (or Kerala Police) has no right to register a case, leave alone investigate it, invoking Section 154 CrPC concerning an offence committed under the IOS Act. The genesis of a case under the IOS Act has to be, necessarily, a complaint in writing by the appropriate government to the competent magistrate under Section 200 CrPC. (Such a complaint never existed in the ISRO espionage case.)

You can't expect the political leadership, mainly occupied by illiterate and semi-literate persons, to know the nuances of law (something even a Magistrate had overlooked). But it could have behaved in a politically sensible manner and should have discontinued playing the absurd techno-legal-political drama after the CBI investigation had nailed the spy case as false with meticulous precision. But neither the CPI (M) nor the Left government headed by Marxist leader E.K. Nayanar was ready to accept the findings of CBI.

The Government of Kerala,[66] withdrew the consent given to CBI under Section 6 of the Delhi Special Police Establishment Act, 1946 and ordered for further investigation by Kerala Police.

The government made the legally and politically immature decision for three reasons.

Firstly, the Marxist Party had used the espionage case to paint Congress leader K. Karunakaran as a traitor. *Desabhimani*, the Marxist mouthpiece, had serialized its version of the espionage

65. It is to be remembered the ISRO espionage case was registered under Sections 3, 4, and 5 of IOS Act.
66. Vide notifications dated 27-6-1996 and 8-7-1996

story featuring all the discharged persons as members of a spy ring as part of the newspaper's political strategy to cash in on the public mood and win the Assembly polls in 1996. The public, who had been fed with so many spicy stories by the combined work of the media, was not ready to accept CBI's conclusion that it was all baseless.

Secondly, CBI had sent to the Chief Secretary of Kerala a confidential report listing out some serious lapses on the part of certain officers of Kerala Police. The government wanted to protect the police officers from possible punishment based on the report.

Thirdly, the police could exercise covert pressure on Chief Minister E.K. Nayanar who was also holding the Home Ministry as there were allegations that his son was involved in a sensational sex scandal, and managed to get an order from the government to further investigate the case with the mala fide intention to somehow prove the absurd espionage case was true, and thereby undo the charges against certain officers in Kerala Police in the confidential report of CBI.

The discharged accused challenged the order of Kerala government before the High court. On 27 November 1996, the Court passed its order[67] thus:

1. The State government has no jurisdiction to file a complaint before a court in respect of any offence under Sections 3, 4, and 5 of the Indian Official Secrets (IOS) Act, in this case.
2. The State, in the exercise of its powers under the Police Act, can direct a police officer to do any further investigation. But, that power, in our opinion, is circumscribed by the provision of the IOS Act.

67. O.P. No. 12747/ 1996

3. It is open to the State government to approach the competent Magistrate having the power to take cognizance in respect of any offence under the IOS Act.

The Court further said, since "the allegation, in this case, being the commission of offences under Sections 3, 4, and 5 of the IOS Act, are connected with a prohibited place, the appropriate Government under Section 13(5) thereof is the Central government. In other words, a Court shall take cognizance of any of the offences under the Act only upon a complaint made by order or under the authority of the Central government. Thus, there can be no doubt that the State of Kerala has no jurisdiction to file a complaint much less to file a report[68] to prosecute the petitioners under Sections 3, 4, and 5 of the IOS Act.

Assuming for the sake of argument that further investigation by the State Police revealed that such an offence had been committed; no competent court shall take cognizance of the same on the basis of any complaint or report by the State Government or its Police organisation."

The court made it clear that the State government cannot approach a court even to file a complaint under the IOS Act with respect to the alleged espionage case in ISRO, a Central government organization, because of the circumscribing provision of the Act.

It is strange that the High Court that ruled so, didn't realize they were considering a case, the very genesis of which was illegal. Why didn't the High Court declare the act of the Magistrate in so far as accepting a report[69] was illegal and the Magistrate passing an order on that report, therefore, was invalid?

---

68. Under S.173 (2) of the CrPC

69. Under Section 173(2)

Interestingly, even CBI that investigated the case for 18 months didn't, at any point, realize it had no legal authority to investigate a case under the IOS Act and file a report of the investigation[70] since neither the Central government nor any agency authorized by the Central government had ever approached the competent Magistrate with a complaint under Section 200 of CrPC, which is mandatory for a case under the IOS Act to exist.

It was crime No.246/94, registered by the Kerala Police that was transferred to CBI through Section 6 notification of the Delhi Special Police Establishment Act, 1946. If the action of Kerala Police was wrong in the light of Section 13(3) and (5) of the IOS Act, under what provision of Law did CBI proceed with the investigation of the same case?

What more, CBI was under the wrong impression that even Kerala Police had the right to register a case under the IOS Act. In its letter[71] addressed to the Chief Secretary, Government of Kerala, the ignorance of CBI vis-à-vis the application and implication of Section 13, which is restrictive, is evident. In one place, the letter reads:

> *The involvement of Raman Srivastava, IGP, was also suspected as per the news items. Despite the lingering suspicions about the conduct of Rasheeda and Fauziya harboured by Kerala Police and the IB officials and the fact that the local Press was playing up the issue and even the name of Raman Srivastava, IGP, was also being linked up with this episode, no immediate steps were taken by the Kerala Police to register a case under the Official Secrets Act and effect the arrest of accused persons, or conduct searches to recover the secret documents and the money, if any, received by the accused*

70. Under Section 173(2) CrPC
71. No. 2783/3/11(S) 94—SIU V/SIC, dated 3 June 1996

as consideration for having passed on the documents/ secrets, or to keep a watch on the activities of the suspected persons.

It is still a legal question how the CJM, Ernakulam, accepted CBI's Closure Report in the light of the High Court's ruling that "there can be no doubt that the State of Kerala has no jurisdiction to file a complaint much less to file a report under S.173 (2) of the Cr. P. C."

The High Court, however, accepted the reality that a legal mistake had been committed by the CJM, Ernakulam when it stated (in Paragraph 22 of the judgment) "Admittedly in this case, the closure report submitted by the CBI has been accepted by the Magistrate."

Even when the judgment categorically stated that Kerala Police have "no jurisdiction to file a complaint much less to file a report"; and that the judicial action of CJM, Ernakulam, accepting the closure report of CBI[72] was not legally right, T. P. Sen Kumar, DIG, entrusted with the job of further investigation, moved the CJM, Thiruvananthapuram (instead of moving the CJM, Ernakulam, who had accepted the Closure Report of CBI), for a formal order to further investigate the case.

The CJM, Thiruvananthapuram, called for all documents from CJM, Ernakulam, and granted permission for further investigation[73].

In the light of the judgment of the High Court, how could the CJM, Thiruvananthapuram, give an order for further investigation under Sec. 173(8)?

After all, 173(8) stems only from 173(2).

How could a magistrate afford to be ignorant of the significance of Section 4 (2) of the Cr.P.C. that reads:

---

72. Under Section 172(2) Cr.P.C.

73. Under section 173 (8) Cr. PC on 13 December 1996

(1) All offences under the Indian Penal Code shall be investigated, inquired into, tried, and otherwise dealt with according to the provisions hereinafter contained; (2) All offences under any other law shall be investigated, inquired into, tried, and otherwise dealt with according to the same provisions, but subject to any enactment for the time being in force regulating the manner or place of investigating, inquiring into, trying or otherwise dealing with such offences.

Read in the context of IOS Act, which is a Special Act, doesn't it sound the CJM was ignorant of the provisions of the law he was dealing with? Or was it a judicial overstepping by the CJM?

Whatever may be the reason, its dimension is better understood when we view it against the backdrop of the Supreme Court judgment on 29 April 1998, quashing Kerala government notification for further investigation.

The duty of the Investigating Agency, the Supreme Court said, is not merely to bolster up a prosecution case with such evidence as may enable the Court to record a conviction but to bring out the real unvarnished truth. Yet, the court observed, "the Kerala government wants the instant case to be further investigated by a team nominated by it with the avowed object of establishing that the accused are guilty, even after the investigating agency of its choice, the CBI found that no case had been made out against them."

This mala fide intention of the Kerala Police is evident from the following passage from the order dated 13 December 1996, passed by the Chief Judicial Magistrate, Thiruvananthapuram, granting permission to Kerala Police to further investigate.

"The report submitted by the Director-General of Police discloses the fact that he has got reliable information that the conclusions arrived at by the CBI during the investigation were not correct. If the case is further investigated, more evidence can be collected which would point towards the guilt of the accused."

The Supreme Court exposed the hidden agenda of the State government thus: "If before taking up further investigation an opinion has already been formed regarding the guilt of the accused and, that too, at a stage when the commission of the offence itself is yet to be proved, it is obvious that the investigation cannot and will not be fair - and its outcome appears to be a foregone conclusion."

The court made it clear that the decision of the Kerala government to further investigate the case was illegal. But the court overlooked the fact that the very genesis of the case they were deciding was illegal and invalid by the legal implication of Sections 13 (3) and (5) of the IOS Act, 1923.

Does it mean the ISRO espionage case had made our system a mad, mad world?

It is interesting to see how the Left government of Kerala responded to the Supreme Court judgment.

Even after getting slapped on the face in public, the Marxist-led Kerala government was in no mood to accept their wrongs. Chief Minister E.K. Nayanar and the then Left Democratic Front Convener V.S. Achuthanandan – both were Politbureau members of the CPI (M) – aired a new theory that the judgment didn't come in their favour because the Central government didn't handle the case properly.

The comrades seemed to have overlooked the fact that the case came up before the Supreme Court during the time of the United Front government at the Centre, remote-controlled by the CPI (M).

More importantly, did the comrades mean the Central Government could have influenced the outcome of the Supreme Court judgment?

21

Discrimination & Cowardice – Quasi Judicial Style

2 May 1996

The CJM, Ernakulam, accepted the Closure Report of the CBI in the ISRO espionage case and discharged all the six accused, including the two Maldivian women. One month later, the CJM discharged all the accused, except D.Sasikumaran, in another connected case the CBI had registered under the Prevention of Corruption Act, 1947.

Though the Chief Judicial Magistrate (CJM), Ernakulam, had granted bail to all the accused in the espionage case, as early on 19 January 1995, the two Maldivian women could not taste freedom for want of sureties. Besides, four defamation cases were pending against Mariam Rasheeda – two against her interview in *India Today* and two against the interview she gave me from the prison for *Savvy*.

However, there was no defamation case against Fauziya Hassan and when the CJM discharged her from the lone pending case registered under the Prevention of Corruption Act, she was free. But the court ordered that her release was conditional. She didn't understand how a release could be conditional when there was no case against her in any courts in India. She collapsed in the accused box.

Within hours, Inspector Vijayan slammed a defamation case against her for an interview she had given to *Asianet TV*. Since there was nobody to take her on bail, Fauziya Hassan had to return to the prison.

It was a clever strategy planned by the State government to hold Fauziya back and executed through Inspector Vijayan with the 'conditional release' order of the CJM, Ernakulam acting as the fait accompli.

The State government wanted to hold back both Mariam Rasheeda and Fauziya Hassan in Kerala since the government was planning to further investigate the case in a desperate attempt to save its police officers from possible legal and official actions in the light of the confidential report the CBI.

▼

3 July 1996

Maitreyan, a social worker, and I sent a joint petition to NHRC to "interfere into the continuous acts of human rights violations by the State government and its police force on the 'accused' even after CBI had closed the case as false and baseless.

NHRC asked the Kerala DGP to report back to the Commission though the petition had made DGP the fourth respondent. DGP asked T.P. Senkumar, DIG, to prepare the report for NHRC.

Interestingly, T.P. Senkumar was the police officer handpicked by Kerala government to investigate the case further to 'prove' that the espionage did take place. Now, the same DIG gets a rare opportunity to investigate for and against the accused!

In a different sense, for and against the human right violators!

Maitreyan and I refused to adduce evidence before the DIG, who was playing conflicting roles with absolutely no conflict. We brought it to the notice of the NHRC. But the Commission overlooked the blatant violation of natural justice.

Meanwhile, Mariam Rasheeda and Fauziya Hassan had filed a joint petition before NHRC citing the violation of human rights they had to face at the hands of Kerala Police and IB. They requested NHRC to allow them to be heard. NHRC, however, didn't take evidence from the Maldivian women.

On 11 December 1996, Fauziya Hassan was discharged from a defamation case, the lone case pending against her. She was a free bird now and could have returned to her country. But the government invoked National Security Agency (NSA) within hours of the court discharging her and detaining her. Significantly, NSA was invoked on Fauziya after two years of her arrest.

Maitreyan and I alerted the NHRC about the black law being clamped on a foreign woman after CBI had found her innocent in the espionage case and the court had discharged her, and even when her petition was pending before the NHRC. But NHRC closed the file, stating that it "cannot examine the validity of the NSA Order" and suggested, "It is open to the aggrieved party to challenge the order before the High Court".

NSA is a preventive detention tool, meant to prevent a possible offender from doing any crime that would affect the security of the nation. The case against Fauziya Hassan was that she, along with others, had spied out secrets from India. How could the same person be an offender and a potential offender at the same time?

But NHRC chose to overlook the patently overt violation of human rights.

If NHRC cannot examine the validity of an NSA order, how could the same NHRC make a hue and cry when film star Sanjay Dutt was detained under Terrorist and Disruptive Activities (Prevention) Act (TADA)?

Maybe, the issue of human rights changes with the status of the persons involved.

Closing the file, NHRC wrote: *The Maldivian women were involved in an espionage case. The case was investigated by the CBI and based on their report, the magistrate ordered their discharge. The said order is now challenged before the High Court, and is pending consideration.*

Where did NHRC get this information from? How did NHRC put on record that the order of the Magistrate discharging the accused has been challenged? There was no case before the High court challenging the order of the Magistrate. What was challenged before the High Court was the notification issued by Kerala government to further investigate the case, and a Division Bench had passed its orders on the petitions on 27 November 1996.

NHRC was telling a lie. Its letter is dated 15 January 1997. As of that day, no case connected with the ISRO espionage case was pending before the High Court. The court had dismissed all the cases on 27 November 1996.

Was it not possible for the NHRC to get correct information regarding the legal status of an issue based on which it closed a file? How could the NHRC rely on the report filed by the DGP and close the file without doing its homework when the petition before the NHRC was about human rights violations by the State, including the State police, and when the DGP was the fourth respondent in the petition?

Most importantly, Mariam Rasheeda was accused in two criminal cases. The overstay case in which the CJM, Ernakulam, had acquitted Mariam Rasheeda on 14 November 1995 on grounds that she was not overstaying, made it clear that Inspector Vijayan had prevented her from leaving India and then booked a case of overstay against her. Why did NHRC turn a blind eye towards this human rights violation?

NHRC advised Mariam Rasheeda and Fauziya Hassan to submit documentary evidence before the High Court if their human rights had been violated.

If so, why should there be a National Human Rights Commission at all?

It is interesting that the same NHRC gave specific directions to Kerala government when S. Nambi Narayanan, co-accused in the espionage case, approached it, overlooking the very same reasons it had cited to dismiss Fauzia Hassan's petition.

The NHRC web page reads:

> *After the conclusion of the criminal case against the complainant, he (Nambi Narayanan) submitted a complaint on 14 October 1998 to NHRC, complaining of gross violation of his human rights and seeking an award of compensation. The complainant, a senior scientist of considerable repute, whose contribution in Space Research was acknowledged, was kept under suspension for a period of 18 months on a false case foisted on him which resulted in the loss of his reputation apart from the ignominy and damage to his health in addition to the considerable expenditure incurred to defend himself from the false accusation. The Commission felt that the damage done to the complainant and his family as a result of the unlawful acts was difficult to fully assess...*
>
> *Thus the Commission on 6 September 1999 directed the Union Home Secretary, Director, IB, Chief Secretary and DGP, Kerala to immediately conduct enquiries to identify the officers who had committed the excesses and initiate appropriate disciplinary as well as criminal action against them and submit a compliance report to the Commission.*

The Commission then, on 4 September 2000, issued notice to the Ministry of Home Affairs as well as the Government of Kerala to show cause as to why immediate interim relief under Section 18(3) of the Protection of Human Rights Act, 1993 be not granted in favour of Shri S. Nambi Narayanan.

In response, the Government of India, as well as the Government of Kerala, appeared before the Commission through their counsel to submit their objections. According to the counsel for the Government of India, a Civil Suit has been filed by the complainant claiming damage amounting to one crore rupees against the State of Kerala and the Union of India, the outcome which would be prejudiced by the award of relief by the Commission.

Also, the matter was subjudice and so the Commission should not grant any such relief. It was also urged that disciplinary proceedings were pending against the charge-sheeted IB officers, the outcome of which might also get prejudiced by the Commission's directions. The counsel for the State of Kerala had contended that the complaint had been made more than one year after the alleged violation of human rights and thus barred from the purview of the NHRC.

The Commission disposed of the objections raised, expressing the view that the Civil Suit would determine the precise terms of the monetary compensation to which the complainant was entitled. It then directed that the sum of Rs 10 lakhs should be paid to S. Nambi Narayanan by the Government of Kerala as `immediate interim relief'. The amount is to be paid within two months and compliance reported to the Commission. The state of Kerala has also been directed to report the action taken against its delinquent officers as directed by the Commission on 6 September 1999.

It is clear the NHRC showed preferential treatment not just to a Bollywood film star but also towards an ISRO- technocrat and a co-accused in the espionage case. So, it dismissed the joint petition filed by two Maldivian women, while they were in prison for nearly three years, raising certain technical points, but passed orders when Nambi Narayanan filed a petition.

How can NHRC justify its discriminatory stand and double standard while considering petitions of human rights violations?

Remember, the NHRC was chaired by a retired Chief justice of India!

▼

23 July 1997

Mariam Rasheeda approached Kerala State Women's Commission (KSWC) as the last ray of hope when somebody in Viyyur Prison had told her the Chairperson of KSWC, a poetess, was humane. But that somebody was unaware the same poetess had stated, "spies should be shot dead".

Mariam Rasheeda moved two separate petitions before the KSWC. The first petition was to initiate prosecution proceedings against Inspector Vijayan who had detained her illegally after she asked the Inspector to get out of her room when he tried to molest her. She produced a copy of her acquittal order by the CJM, Ernakulam, in the overstay case, a judicial proof to establish that her detention for twenty-two days since her arrest on 20 October 1994, was illegal. The petition also said how she was stripped naked by the interrogators while in custody, and how they had molested her.

The second petition sought the Commission's help to take her on bail since there was nobody to stand as her surety. Her judicial custody since 2 May 1996, after the court had discharged her from the espionage case, was for the sole reason that Inspector Vijayan had filed two defamation cases against her for daring to tell the media that she was a victim of his sexual frustration. She didn't get anybody to stand as surety in a bailable offence, the maximum punishment for which is two years.

On 18 August 1997, four Commission members led by its Chairperson went to Viyyur Prison to take evidence.

"We do not feel the Maldivian women should be put in jail inordinately just because they are foreign nationals. They are remaining in jail because they don't have the financial backup to pay the bail money," a visibly shattered Chairperson told the media after the Commission took evidence from both Mariam Rasheeda and Fauziya Hassan.

A week later, the Commission decided to seek the release of the Maldivian women. The Commission "is only looking at the issue from the human rights angle and the priority now is to get the women released."

The Commission then informed the Press that it had sent a report to the Chief Secretary of the State "seeking the release of the Maldivian women within thirty days, failing which the Commission would move the court".

It was the peak. After evading serious issues and creating a media blitz by majoring in on minor issues, the KSWC decided to go for the plunge on a highly sensitive matter.

But the efforts of KSWC were thwarted by Chief Minister E.K. Nayanar. At the press briefing after the cabinet meeting, a visibly annoyed E.K. Nayanar thundered that he would not permit "any Commission – women's Commission or men's Commission – to meddle with this issue".

The Commission didn't react to the snub.

On 6 September 1996, the Sessions Court of Thiruvananthapuram granted unconditional bail to Mariam Rasheeda in all defamation cases against her. But Mariam was apprehensive. She feared she would be booked under NSA – the same way the government detained Fauziya Hassan when she was discharged from all other cases. Mariam moved for anticipatory bail. Rejecting her application, the court ordered, "The Public Prosecutor has submitted that there is no case against the petitioner and that the petitioner's apprehension of arrest is unreal."

But her apprehensions proved right. Within hours of her release, the State government faxed her detention order under NSA to the office of District Collector, Thrissur, where she was kept in the Viyyur jail.

The Public Prosecutor fooled the judiciary. The State government headed by the Marxist leader E.K. Nayanar hacked the humane vibes in Marxism.

All these developments happened after the KSWC took notice of the case. The next day, the Commission aired a new story: "We couldn't interfere because it has now gone beyond the State jurisdiction. We were planning to do something. Now it is beyond our jurisdiction. We have informed the National Women's Commission. We hope the National Commission would take up the issue."

Lies. Salted lies.

KSWC clearly succumbed under pressure from IB. Two senior IB officials visited the Commission when it was deliberating the issue, and warned the Commission of serious consequences. The Commission toned down its letter to the Chief Secretary and sent it through its secretary without making any entry in the Commission records. The incorrigible Chief Minister lashed out at the Commission at a press conference, and the Chief Secretary asked the Commission to take the letter back, even before it was entered in the register.

What a farce!

NHRC and KSWC knew pretty well that if they wanted to book anybody for human rights violations connected with the espionage case, it was not Inspector Vijayan, a small fry; not a recalcitrant editor; not the callous Press; not the misguided comrades who ruled the state; not the SIT of Kerala Police composed mostly of flat-footed cops; but the IB – stamping its signature on the rogue's gallery.

Part - VI

The Victims

22

Soliloquy

. . .03. . .02. . .01. . .

The nation was counting its heartbeats. Only a fraction of a second was needed for the maiden operational flight to inject the in-house satellite into the low earth polar sun-synchronous orbit using the indigenously developed launcher; the prelude to going commercial.

The countdown began the previous day, 28 September 1997. The launch was scheduled for 10:20 a.m. The azure sky appeared like a pilot's dream.

At 10:10 a.m., the master computer at Sriharikota Range (SHAR)[74], six kilometres away from the launch pad, took the reins, advanced the critical time by three minutes and finished the countdown.

. . .00.

Electric current was passed through the squib. It exploded with a very high velocity, igniting the charge zone in the core stage. The splash ignited the solid propellant, a mixture of Ammonium Perchlorate and HTPB that binds the oxidizing agent, fuel, and other ingredients into a solid but elastic mass. Four of the six strap-on boosters were also ignited.

A blast. A blaze. A roar.

---

74. Renamed as Satish Dhawan Space Centre in 2002

PSLV-C 1, the 240 tonnes, 44.43-m tall launch vehicle with four stages, carrying IRS-1D satellite, penetrated through the unseen layers of the spotless sky, leaving plumes of white smoke for ordinary eyes. The rest was there on the computer monitor at SHAR.

The first stage separated after 119 seconds and the Vikas engine, an indigenously developed liquid propulsion system using Viking technology, ignited. The vehicle cleared the dense atmosphere 40 seconds later. At a height of 128 km, the heat shield separated. At 282 seconds, the second stage separated and the third, solid, ignited. At 501 km, the third too separated. Then the vehicle coasted for 101 seconds before the fourth stage ignited. 437 seconds later, the last stage, the liquid, separated. The 1200 kg remote sensing satellite was then injected into the polar sun-synchronous orbit, 817 km above the earth, designed to complete one orbit around the planet every 101.35 minutes.

Millions of Indians watched the green blip on their TV monitor gliding smoothly along a red line – the predetermined trajectory, with copybook precision.

A select few had the privilege to watch the whole thing on the computer screen inside the control room. One among the elite class was Prime Minister Inder Kumar Gujral. In his usual style, Gujral caressed his Bulganin, a residue of his ambassadorial days in Moscow. The media-savvy Prime Minister then reached out from his seat to remove a glass and flower vase to help the lensmen click his glee clean.

Gujral embraced ISRO Chairman K. Kasturirangan, who was in tears.

Success makes you so ecstatic that you cry.

▼

29 September 1997

Sitting in his office in Anthareeksha Bhavan, ISRO Head-Quarters, Bangalore, S. Nambi Narayanan was watching the success on his TV monitor. In the morning, he had gone to a temple to pray for the success of the launch. Then it was a couple of disturbing hours at the office. Rooms close to his office remained closed. The Chairman and Prof U.R. Rao, Space Commission member, had gone to SHAR. At that corner of the complex, he, the Director of Advanced Technology and Planning was alone. Forlorn.

He lit a cigarette the moment the fourth stage ignited. It was his blood and sweat. His phone rang. A disturbing call...

He took a deep puff and blew it out of his nose. It went out through the door, orbited the complex, and headed towards the plumes of white smoke still hanging around in the sky.

Where had it gone wrong? Why an apogee of 817 and a perigee of 300?

A flash of lightning. A thunder. It was going to rain.

The lightning gave a flash to the rocket man, the cue to begin with. The rocket had failed to achieve the required incremental velocity; the reason why it struck a lower perigee.

But why did that happen?

Two options, he started the analysis. Some of the stages had underperformed. Or the fourth stage had malfunctioned.

Now which among the two possibilities had worked against the system?

To get a clue, he asked for the pressure-time graphs of the fourth stage tanks. He scanned the graphs which gave him an input that the gas meant to pressurize the tank had met with a leak for about ten seconds. And then the leak stopped miraculously.

He got the cause of the leak. And the cause of the miraculous stoppage of the leak.

Yes, it could stop if the leak was through a relief valve. Nothing miraculous about it! Everything was scientific and pre-designed.

The regulator, downstream the gas tank, had malfunctioned. The relief valve opened automatically to save the system. By the time the regulator started functioning properly, the relief valve closed, automatically. However, in the process, the fourth stage lost some gas which ultimately led to the loss of incremental velocity. Hence a lower perigee.

He rose from his seat, took a piece of chalk, and drew the flow diagram of the fourth stage on a board fixed to the wall behind his seat.

The puzzle was solved. But he couldn't solve a larger puzzle; the enigmatic one. The bolt that reduced him to a shell.

▼

Nambi Narayanan lit another cigarette, then another and another... He heard footsteps closing in. The smell of Panama cigarette filled the room. But he smokes only Wills.

Through the smokescreen of painful memories, he saw an image – 5' 11", dark-complexioned man with a flat nose.

Mr A.

Then he was caught in an avalanche. In that microsecond, before he was thrown into the aching orbit of technological absurdity, he heard the voice of a slap. He felt its pain. His saliva tasted blood.

He was sitting in the guest house of Hindustan Latex Ltd., Thiruvananthapuram. Mr A smoked Panama continuously and quoted the Bible intermittently. Mr B, a grey-haired black guy with a sharp nose, took notes. He was shorter than Mr A. Definitely, a subordinate to the Panama billboard.

Mr A gave a fantastic tribute to him. He never thought so many adjectives could suffix his name. And then he fired his first salvo.

"Why did you do this?"

"What?"

"This espionage."

"What espionage?"

"Mr Nambi Narayanan... Oh, I am sorry. Dr S. Nambi Narayanan, Project Director, Cryogenic System Project; Associate Project Director, GSLV, Deputy Director, Liquid Propulsion Systems Centre. . . and what else?"

"Many more. But, I don't have that Dr prefixed to my name. You seem to have been misled."

"That's okay. You are as good as a doctor. But, tell me why did you do this crime?"

"What crime are you talking about?"

"Bullshit! If you tell on your own, it will be good for you. Otherwise..."

"Still you haven't told what the crime is."

"Bastard, you don't know? Then hear. You have sold the nation's secrets and technology. I mean, rocket technology, to Pakistan. We have proof. Now we want to hear from you. Tell us! Tell us, you rascal, what all things have been spied out to Pakistan? How much money have you earned by selling your country to the enemy?"

A team of four persons entered the room.

Mr C, a frail and short guy whose face belied his age; Mr D, a tall, medium built in his late 40s with a burn-mark on his left neck; Mr E, a thirty-plus young man, fair, medium built; and Mr F, a bald old man in a safari suit.

Mr C introduced Mr F as top brass in the Intelligence Bureau.

So these are the wise men of IB, Nambi Narayanan thought. But why should they talk nonsense?

Mr C, who had a lot of pimple pits on his face, yelled, "Bastard, do you know the charges against you?"

"No!"

He pulled a sheet of paper from his red plastic folder and read out the charges. Nambi Narayanan felt he was listening to a new generation cock and bull story.

"Our boss has to return to Delhi today itself to brief the Prime Minister. You better tell everything," Mr C read out the epilogue.

"I have nothing to tell you except that I don't understand what you are talking about. This must be a misunderstanding. Your story sounds like an absurd drama."

The new members looked at each other and left the room in two minutes. Mr A took the bridle.

"We understand things properly. Tell me when did you meet those bitches?"

"Who?"

"Mariam Rasheeda and Fauziya Hassan."

"Never."

"How dare you say that? They have told us everything. Even about your perversions. Come on, speak out! We shall spare you if you accept everything. Otherwise. . . We will bring your ass out through your mouth."

"Please believe me. I don't know these women. I have never met them. What do you mean by everything?"

"If you continue to fool us we will bring Fauziya here. She will slap you with her chappals. That photo will appear on all papers tomorrow. Do you want us to do that?"

"I can't help it. But can you get such photographs published? Do you have that rapport with the Press? Now I understand how the newspapers carry interrogation stories every day."

"It is none of your business." A new voice. Mr B! So, he was not dumb.

"Sasikumaran has confessed everything."

"Did he? What did he say?"

"So you are worried? Fine! He said you have sold documents to Pakistan. He said dollars have changed hands. He said about your meetings with the spies in Madras, and Bangalore... What else?"

"I don't know what Sasi might have told you. But, please believe me; rocketry cannot be transferred through drawings. For instance, we spent nearly 135 man-years in France, under a legal contract, to acquire the Viking technology. I was the team leader. We had worked with the French team. We had first-hand information on all aspects of training. And then we got the engine and its technology. Despite all this, it took more than fourteen years to fabricate the engine. It was successfully used seventeen years after we acquired the technology. It is just not possible to transfer rocket technology through drawings. Nobody will buy them."

"So, you gave them free!" Mr A changed track.

"I never said so. I was trying to convince you that you can't spy rocketry through documents."

"Why not? If Pakistan wants to duplicate Viking engine, they can do so with the help of drawings."

"You can do nothing with the drawings."

"You mean the drawings are useless?"

"I said drawings are not sufficient. Again, why should one go for spying technology when it can be bought for money from the same country? Yes, I mean it. You can buy these technologies for a price."

Mr A looked at Mr B and whispered something into his subordinate's ear. Mr B shook his head and went towards the window. He opened it. Fresh air gushed in. Mr A lit another Panama and asked, "To whom did you transfer the cryogenic missile technology?"

"Cryogenic missile technology!" Nambi Narayanan couldn't help laughing aloud. "You are confused, Mr... Sorry, I don't know your name."

"You need not know."

"Okay! No country in the world uses cryogenic technology in a missile. You need a minimum of forty-eight hours to fill the propellant. It is too complex. Too expensive. And how can India transfer the cryo engine technology to anybody? We are yet to acquire it. Believe me sir, you have been misled."

There was total silence, except for the occasional chirp of a bird, the bark of a dog, the horn of a passing car.

"Can I meet DIG Siby Mathews?" Nambi Narayanan broke the silence.

"Why should you meet him? It is enough that you tell us."

"I want to meet him. I think I can convince him. This is cruel."

"You need not try to convince him. He is convinced that you are a traitor, bastard." Mr A squeezed the butt of his Panama under his shoes. He took a new one. He offered one to Nambi. He took from his pant pocket a cute red lighter, lighted Nambi's cigarette before he lit his. Nambi took a puff. He felt relieved.

"Where were you on 24 January?" Mr A moved closer to him. He rested his right toe on Nambi's chair.

"I don't remember."

"You have to. You cannot forget that date. You are known for your sharp memory."

"Will you please tell me where you were last Friday?" Nambi felt a bit irritated to see Mr A placing his toe on his seat.

"Don't ask questions. Just give answers."

"Yes, but be reasonable. You are asking where I had been on a particular day some ten months ago. You don't remember a particular day unless that is very important for you. Such as your birthday, marriage anniversary..."

Something suddenly pulled Nambi's memory line back. It stood frozen at a point. A funeral...

"Yes, I remember. On 23 January, Manikantan, one of my close friends, died. I had attended the funeral that evening. The next day, I went to my office. The vehicle logbook would tell you that. I had signed some purchase files on that day. On 25th January, I celebrated the first birth anniversary of my granddaughter. I had invited nearly a hundred persons to my home."

The interrogator turned silent. Mr A pulled his toe back from Nambi's chair. This time he threw the butt out through the window.

A car came close to the guesthouse. The driver applied its brake. Its doors were flung open. Mr F was escorted into the car, and the white Ambassador sped away.

"Okay okay. Now, when did you first meet Abdul Qadeer Khan?" Mr A had another cigarette on his lips.

"Who is that?"

"Don't act, Nambi. We know you are a good actor. Dr Abdul Qadeer Khan is a well-known nuclear scientist. He came, met you and struck a deal for the transfer of rocket technology. That was sometime in 1988. Now, can you remember who Dr Abdul Khan is? And, tell us the rest."

"I don't know Dr Abdul Khan. What you have told about me is a lie. But, tell me, what has a nuclear scientist got to do with rocketry? Again, if India plans to do espionage in Pakistan, will we send Prof U.R. Rao or Dr Abdul Kalam for the job? You send only an unknown man, isn't it?"

"You are right. We agree. So who was that unknown spy from Pakistan?"

Nambi smelt a rat. They were framing up a story. They were making course corrections. He found himself helping them to fabricate a crime story against him. He decided to keep silent.

"Mr Nambi," Mr A said, "If you think you are smart, we are smarter. We have more than twenty-five years' experience in handling spies like you. We pray for our daily bread, whereas you bastards amass so much of wealth and sell the country. Come on, tell us the names! You can't keep mum before an interrogator."

Nambi felt another blow on his face.

▼

Nambi Narayanan felt hungry. He badly wanted a drink or two. He took his diary and searched for a faded black and white photograph inside. It was there.

Young and slim, Nambi Narayanan was all smiles. He was standing opposite Mrs Indira Gandhi. To her left was Dr Vikram Sarabhai.

"He is my Princetonian," Sarabhai told Mrs Gandhi.

That was immediately after the young scientist S. Nambi Narayanan returned from the USA. In 1969, three years after joining ISRO, Nambi Narayanan obtained a NASA fellowship. At that time, Indian rocket engineers were working on 75 mm diameter D-1 rockets meant for injecting copper needles into the outer atmosphere for gathering some basic data.

He joined for his Masters' Programme in Chemical Rocket Propulsion in Princeton University under Prof Luggi Crocoo, who was involved in the American Liquid Propulsion Programme. There, he became the first Indian to study the liquid system. He passed the two-year course in nine-and-a-half months and got the rare opportunity to visit all the leading aerospace centres in America, thanks to a letter of introduction from Prof Crocco.

Back home, instead of joining the SLV programme, which was using solid propellant, Nambi Narayanan started developing the liquid propulsion system from scratch. Within two years, he succeeded in injecting the fuel and oxidiser kept separately, into one chamber. They burnt and expanded through a nozzle heralding the liquid days of Indian rocketry.

It was around this time Dr Sarabhai introduced him to Mrs Gandhi as his Princetonian.

▼

The Director of Advanced Technology and Planning descended the steps. People who had come to see the exhibition of rocket models were still hanging around. After all, you feel euphoric when your national pride flies high.

But what about the man who had helped that pride fly high? He got crushed under the buckled shoes of a multi-layer conspiracy which ranges from the sexual frustration of a circle inspector over a Maldivian woman's refusal to share a bed with him to a commercial conspiracy hatched at the international level to puncture the space elan of ISRO and to kick India out of the elite circuit of space oligopoly.

The road from Anthareeksha Bhavan to Bangalore city is not that busy. You can even spot a couple of bullock carts rolling gently along the route to the rocket headquarters. As the official car taking Nambi Narayanan back to his quarters negotiated a curve, he saw a police jeep coming out of Sadasivanager Police Station. It had a couple of men dressed in plain clothes at the rear escorting a man in handcuff.

▼

1 December 1994

The jeep was coming out of the court of Additional CJM, Thiruvananthapuram, after Nambi Narayanan was remanded to police custody. Vanchiyoor Police Station, where he had slept on a bench the previous night, was very close to the courtroom. Lensmen were vying with one another to click him. A constable suggested him to cover his face with a towel.

"Why should I?" Nambi Narayanan asked the constable and requested the driver to hold for a moment to make sure that all the photographers had their share of the 'exclusive'.

As the jeep crossed the police station, he saw three familiar faces. Advocate Gopinathan, and his two brothers-in-law. Then he saw Chandran on his scooter, looking all around to locate him. He wanted to wave his hands to Chandran to catch his attention. But he couldn't. He could see everything, but couldn't react. Something had suddenly gone wrong inside him. He tried to call Chandran. But his voice got choked inside his throat.

"Did you call me, sir?" driver Chandran asked Nambi, slowing down the car.

"I didn't Chandran, I was just thinking," Nambi replied.

Yes, Nambi Narayanan was thinking something which he never wanted anybody to know.

23

The Fall

17 December 1994

End of a journey. How boring it was!

Fifteen hours to travel 315 km!

Guruvayoor–Thiruvananthapuram road is not a safari track. It is National Highway 47, the nation's pride.

And he was not on a bullock cart.

Fan-belt was the first to go. Then the clutch turned unruly. The wiper went into a coma. The left tyre at the rear burst due to under-inflation.

The rainy Friday night of that wintry December appeared like a nightmare for Raman Srivastava, Inspector General of Police.

He had gone to Guruvayoor Sreekrishna temple, a practice he has been continuing on the first day of every Malayalam month for more than two decades. The Uttar Pradesh man knew the Malayalam calendar better than many Keralites.

It was past midnight. He was dead tired and badly needed hours of undisturbed sleep. He asked his wife Anjali not to disturb him and gave direction to his camp office not to connect any calls to him.

Next morning, at 8:47 a.m. a call reached the camp office. The IG's personal security had to disobey him. The call was connected to him.

"Reach Malligai today itself."

"Can I make it tomorrow?" a visibly tired Srivastava pleaded, "I am dead tired."

"No. Take the evening flight. I tried to contact your DGP. I couldn't. Please inform him also."

At the other end of the line was M.L. Sharma, Joint Director of CBI. He was speaking from Malligai, CBI's interrogation centre at Chennai.

Raman Srivastava booked a seat by the evening flight and confirmed to M.L. Sharma that he was coming.

He tried to sleep after that, but couldn't.

What is wrong with my stars? He looked at his rings. Four in total. The latest one was to guard him against the wicked smile of a newborn star at the apogee of the cosmos. But neither the super cop who holds the record of becoming the youngest IG in the country nor his astrologer who could keep a deadly star at bay realized that the Press in Kerala was even more powerful.

Srivastava scanned *The Indian Express* to see whether the paper had printed a new lie on him. Two weeks back, it had front-paged an 'exclusive' about his links with the spy ring. The story was planted by the IB officials. And now, with a legal forum in Kochi moving the High Court seeking his arrest, the newspapers were celebrating the highly explosive spy story.

▼

Operation Srivastava began on 22 October 1994 with *Kerala Kaumudi*, a Malayalam newspaper, linking his name to the spy ring for the sole reason that its Editor M.S. Mani found it the right opportunity to take revenge on the IG.

In no time, the terror of the Kerala Police became the whipping boy of the media. The symphony reached its crescendo with *The Indian Express* filing a front-page story with a screaming headline,

'Net Closing in on Top Police Official', describing Raman Srivastava as a member of the spy ring, receiving and delivering highly sensitive defence secrets.

His father, a retired IG, advised him not to take anything lying down. And Srivastava decided to take the bull by its horn. He typed out his press statement and approached the DGP for formal permission to go to the Press. The DGP fully agreed with the IG. With his letter, Srivastava met the Chief Secretary. He asked the IG to wait till the Chief Minister returned from his tour.

But before the Chief Minister returned, CBI had landed in Thiruvananthapuram and Srivastava found it improper to issue a statement then. He informed the Chief Secretary and sent in a formal letter withdrawing his request to go to the Press.

'What new things have emerged?' Raman Srivastava asked the question again and again while on the flight. The CBI officers had questioned him twice before M.L. Sharma summoned him to Malligai.

He watched the wings cruising through the mountain-like clouds.

What could Anjali be doing now? Might have returned to the *pooja* room. Before he had left for Malligai, she had put her arms around him and whispered, almost breaking down, "Whatever happens, you have to come back to us."

She feared he would commit suicide out of shame.

The seat walet had a couple of newspapers and magazines. He didn't touch them. Not even the glossy ones. All are trash. Of late, he had developed distaste for what they called journalism.

He had nothing else to do. How long can you watch the wing and clouds? He tried to take a nap. He closed his eyes. His memories woke up.

▼

5 December 1994

It was his first encounter with the CBI team. Srivastava reached the CRPF camp in Thiruvananthapuram in his private car at 3:30 p.m.

M.L. Sharma and his deputy P.M. Nair met him at the officers' mess. He had heard of Sharma as a tough guy in charge of the terrorist cell in CBI. Their questions were not focussed. They had taken up the case only the previous day.

But six days later, it was not the same experience. At the State Bank of Travancore Guest House, Thiruvananthapuram, the grilling was on in full swing. This time it was R.C. Sharma and Ashok Kumar, both Superintendents of CBI.

The tough face of R.C. Sharma, the sharp eyes of Ashok Kumar and their razor-like questions linking him to Fauziya Hassan, two ISRO scientists, a businessman and Mariam Rasheeda came rushing on him.

He heard Mariam Rasheeda's name for the first on 20 October around 3 p.m. when Police Commissioner V.R. Rajeevan, DIG, gave him a call and told him the Maldivian woman had been overstaying and that IB, RAW and Special Branch had questioned her because they had some doubts about her. Srivastava, Rajeevan's immediate boss, agreed with his suggestion that she could be booked for overstay.

Two days later, *Kerala Kaumudi* front-paged a report linking his name to Mariam Rasheeda who, the newspaper reported, was a spy. In the light of the report, he told the DGP and Commissioner that he was distancing himself from the investigation which, otherwise, he should have supervised.

"I haven't met any one of them," Srivastava's reply didn't seem that convincing to R.C. Sharma.

"Not at Hotel Lucia or Madras International?"

"I have been to Lucia. Its owner is my friend. But not to Madras International. At Lucia, I didn't see any of the accused."

"You saw them at the Army Club in Bangalore?"

"I have never been there."

"Do you occasionally wear a coat?"

"I don't have one. I normally wear a safari suit or shirt and pants. I used warm clothes only during my posting in Shillong."

"What about Nambi Narayanan? You have been to his house any number of times."

"I don't know him, but I can identify him. I have seen his photos in the papers. Maybe he can also identify me. My photos also have appeared in newspapers. I am a known face in Thiruvananthapuram."

"How come all of them claim they know you?"

"Could be a conspiracy against me."

"Who are the conspirators?"

"I don't know who exactly they are. I have many enemies."

"Like who?"

Srivastava smiled. What a long list! "Maybe," he said, "Mathew John of IB has some grudge against me. Or else why should he threaten the DGP that he would book me under the NSA?"

"You mean, an IB officer had threatened your DGP?" Sharma sounded excited. He pushed his chair closer to the table and leaned forward a bit more. And Srivastava narrated the episode.

"Did Fauziya give you nine lakh US dollars?"

"No."

"What about your joint venture with Sasikumaran and Chandrasekhar to set up a factory for bulletproof vests?"

"I have no business. I don't know either of the two."

"The three of you have invested four crore rupees as advance for a deep-sea fishing vessel that costs more than fourteen crores!"

"My god!"

"What weapons do you possess?"

"In 1981, I bought a .22 rifle from Singapore. I sold that to Thrissur Armory for eight thousand rupees. I had also purchased one pistol from the government and sold it for three thousand."

"What about your .30 US rifle?"

"My papa got it while he was the IG of Arunachal Pradesh. It was gifted to me. I still keep it. I have a license for it. Besides, my wife and I hold two 12 bore guns and one .410 bore gun. All are licensed."

▼

The plane touched the runway, ran for a while, and stopped. Srivastava looked at his watch. It was 8:05 p.m. 'Now, what could be the sudden provocation for CBI to summon me to Malligai,' he thought. The only solace was that M.L. Sharma sounded mild over the phone.

P.M. Nair, DIG, CBI, asked his aide to clear Srivastava's bag and took the IG straight from the tarmac in an Indian Airlines jeep towards the rear, from where they got into an official car of the CBI and drove towards Malligai, neatly fooling a battalion of lensmen and scribes led by a DIG of the IB. They were waiting at the arrival lounge to flash that Srivastava had been taken to Malligai for interrogation.

The white Ambassador car entered the fortified and floodlit campus and drove past the machinegun-wielding security men before it slowed down and stopped at the portico of a huge, old-fashioned bungalow.

Srivastava was escorted to the front right corner room on the first floor, just above the portico.

"Why sir, what is the sudden reason?" Tension started eating into Srivastava's psyche.

"We are almost heading towards the conclusion. We want to reach the bottom of the story," M.L. Sharma said.

Once again, Srivastava was asked to give his version of the events beginning with the arrest of Mariam Rasheeda.

"Do you know any of the accused personally?" Sharma asked, cutting short his version.

"I don't know any one of them," he said.

M.L. Sharma looked at P.M. Nair. It was a signal. The door opened. A fair-skinned, bearded man walked in.

Yes, the guy! Srivastava thought for a moment. Why should this pious-looking man betray his country?

"Do you know him?" Sharma posed the question to the bearded man.

"No," he sounded shattered inside.

"And you?" this time, the question was to Srivastava.

"Yes, Nambi Narayanan. I have seen his photographs."

"That's all?"

"Yes."

"Next," Sharma said. Another bearded man. He had a long beard and equally long hair. Then a stout guy. And then a dark and middle-aged man. They came one by one.

Srivastava couldn't identify them. Nor could they.

"And next."

A fair old lady came to the room.

"No," Srivastava said.

"And do you know him?" P.M. Nair directed the question to her.

"No."

"Then why did you all say before the IB men that you know him well?" Both Sharma and Nair looked visibly annoyed.

"Never," Nambi Narayanan interrupted. "I was tortured just because I didn't agree to say three names – Prof U.R. Rao, Dr A.E. Muthunayagam and Raman Srivastava."

Raman Srivastava looked at Nambi Narayanan with gratitude. The broken technocrat felt a touch of solace from an unknown heart.

The other three men said they were tortured to such an extent that they finally said in front of the video camera that Srivastava was a member of the spy ring.

And then entered the queen bee.

"He is Raman Srivastava," she told M.L. Sharma.

Srivastava's heartbeat stopped. His throat went dry. He saw the face of Anjali, Jitu and Ritu. Is the worst going to happen? My god! Then he heard her voice.

"Inspector Vijayan had shown me his photos, both in uniform and mufti. I was given training to identify his photograph from among other photographs. They nearly broke my knee when I resisted."

Srivastava couldn't believe her words. *The same Vijayan who had rushed to my home and said she had mentioned my name to IB,* he thought.

But he had stopped believing the world around him. In the labyrinthine corridors of existence made of lies and half-truths, he had lost track of the corridors and their turns.

The identification parade was over. M.L. Sharma asked Srivastava that he should, on his return, fax to his number V.R. Rajeevan's letter to the DGP sent four days after the arrest of Mariam Rasheeda. Srivastava didn't know the letter had more than enough ammunition to blast the spy ring theory.

The worst had ended. Srivastava shared dinner, brought from the mess, with M.L. Sharma. It was 10:30 p.m. Five minutes later, he got a call from his son Jitu.

"Nothing special," Srivastava consoled his son.

"Who do you think has framed you?" Sharma asked Srivastava, both lighting cigarettes after a light dinner.

"I think I was initially implicated by *Kerala Kaumudi*." Srivastava then detailed the editor's enmity towards him.

Sharma gave hints that he had been framed.

"Why can't you talk to the DGP over the phone to crack down on the plotters?" Srivastava wanted to know.

Sharma gave an enigmatic smile. He didn't want to tell the IG that both his and the DGP's phones were being tapped by IB.

Early the next morning, Raman Srivastava was taken to the airport. He checked in and was on board an Indian Airlines flight to Thiruvananthapuram.

Again a window seat! Again the wing gliding through the mountain- like clouds!

He scanned *The Indian Express*. From the front page, it screamed: "Raman Srivastava IG was arrested by CBI and taken to Bangalore for interrogation. CBI had planned to take him to Malligai. But then they decided to change the venue."

Why does IB, which leaks news to the press, always err? He threw down the morning lie with utter contempt.

▼

Anjali couldn't believe her eyes. She too had read the report. But here, her man was back! She held his hand firmly.

At times, the story heads for a climax. And then nosedives.

A spirited forum in Kochi filed a writ of mandamus before Kerala High Court, seeking a direction to CBI to arrest Raman Srivastava. The Single Bench dismissed the writ and the forum moved an appeal. The Division Bench ordered CBI to produce all records connected with the questioning of Srivastava and directed the investigating officers to file separate affidavits stating whether there was an iota of evidence to establish even prima facie connection of Srivastava to the spy ring. Not satisfied with the affidavits, the Bench directed CBI Director, K. Vijaya Rama Rao to file an affidavit. The CBI Director's affidavit made it clear, in unambiguous terms, that there was not even an iota of doubt against Raman Srivastava.

▼

13 January 1995

The court was to pronounce its judgment as to whether to direct CBI to arrest Raman Srivastava or not.

Thirteen is an inauspicious number. It evokes memories of the mother of all betrayals and crucifixion of the truth. But Anjali tried to think differently. CBI has cleared her husband from all allegations. She was waiting for the High Court judgment to catch the next flight to Delhi to see her critically ill mother.

She was sipping a cup of black tea when, inside a jam-packed courtroom, 212 km away, a two-member Bench pronounced the judgment.

"The Kerala High Court has dismissed the appeal seeking direction to CBI to arrest Raman Srivastava," the radio news bulletin sounded like a voice from heaven.

"Oh god! You are great." Anjali put her cup on the glass-topped teapoy. Steam was still seeking liberation from the still black liquid.

"No court has the power to direct the investigation officer to include a person as an accused in the case while the investigation is in progress. Before the police file the final report, no court can direct the investigating agency to implicate one as an accused and arrest him." The voice from heaven continued.

Anjali prayed to god with folded hands.

Then the band changed. It was a radio broadcast from hell.

"The Intelligence Bureau, which has its own investigating machinery, in unmistakable terms have found the involvement of Srivastava in the spy ring."

Srivastava looked at his wife. He gazed into the vast expanse of the blue sky. No mountain-like clouds. No wings that blade through the clouds. Then he turned his eyes into the vaster sky within.

He was searching where the bolt came from.

It was a long and frozen time. Nobody uttered a word. The family sat face to face, like a still frame. Night set in. The gunman switched the lights on. But the family didn't feel the light. They were inside a tunnel with both ends closed.

At 12.30, a special messenger threw a bombshell into the tunnel.

Suspension order for Raman Srivastava.

Before Anjali could give a healing touch to her crumbling man, the phone rang. It was her brother from Delhi. Their mother had breathed her last at 12:30.

24

The Liaison Man

18 November 1994

An Indian airlines flight was getting ready from Bangalore airport for its flight to Delhi. A man in his late forties, resembling a disgruntled dropout from the Pune Film Institute, led a Russian group into the security zone. He talked fluent Russian. Cracked Jokes in Russian. Smiled in Russian.

He was K. Chandrasekhar, liaison man of Glavkosmos in India, the Middle East, and the Far East. He was taking a team from Glavkosmos, the Russian space agency, to Delhi to catch the flight to Moscow.

"Ladies and gentlemen, may I have your attention, please. There is a message for the ISRO representative who accompanies the Russian team. Please come to the reception. Urgent." It was one of the many announcements made at the airport.

"What is that?" A.I. Dunayev, Chairman of Glavkosmos, asked.

"Maybe some message for some ISRO man," Chandrasekhar answered.

The security check was over. The Russian team and their liaison man entered the plane. Chandrasekhar looked through the window to see whether some policeman was heading towards the plane.

He knew the announcement was for him. He didn't unlock the safety belt even after the takeoff was over. He apprehended his arrest any time. The plane cruised smoothly. But Chandrasekhar fell into an air pocket.

▼

20 October 1994

Hours before going to bed, Chandrasekhar was sipping whiskey when his phone rang. The man at the other end introduced himself as R.R. Nair from IB. He wanted to meet Chandrasekhar, the next day afternoon.

Sitting in the drawing room of House 466, 4th Main R.M.V., Stage III, Bangalore, R.R. Nair asked Chandrasekhar what Mariam Rasheeda meant to him.

Chandrasekhar had met Mariam Rasheeda for the first time at Thiruvananthapuram when they got adjacent seats on a flight to Bangalore. They chatted and became friends. She told him about Fr. Pinto who was demanding fifty thousand rupees, besides twenty-five thousand rupees already given, for school admission for her friend's daughter in Bangalore.

"He is a cheat," she said and asked whether he knew anybody in Baldwin Girls High School.

He did not know. But the principal's husband, Thomas, was a close friend of Sharma, his long-time friend. Chandrasekhar promised her help. Before the plane touched Bangalore, he gave her his visiting card.

"Mariam Rasheeda called me the next day," Chandrasekhar said.

"Then what happened?" R.R. Nair wanted to know.

"I entrusted the work with Sharma, who managed the admission."

"Then?" R.R. Nair didn't suppress his curiosity.

"Nothing," Chandrasekhar uttered a lie. He didn't tell the IB man that he had made a couple of outings with her and had introduced her to ISRO technocrat D. Sasikumaran, his friend.

R.R. Nair threw a hidden smile at him and left. Chandrasekhar got the meaning of that smile two hours later when V. Sudhakar, Managing Director of KELTEC, phoned him from Thiruvananthapuram. Chandrasekhar was expecting that call to know about the progress in the proposed joint venture between Glavkosmos and KELTEC to fabricate cryogenic engines for ISRO.

But Sudhakar didn't talk business. He signalled danger. Quoting *Desabhimani*, Sudhakar informed him about the arrest of Mariam Rasheeda and the shocking information that she had been spying for Pakistan.

Chandrasekhar deciphered the hidden meaning in the sarcastic smile of the IB man. He tried to drown the shock in three pegs of whiskey.

"Veg or non-veg?"

"No thanks," he said to the air hostess. He wanted to go to the washroom. For that, he had to unlock his seat belt. But he didn't dare to. It was his safety belt. He pressed his back firmly on the pushback, closed his eyes, and tried to cut his memory line. He succeeded.

For a while, he was alone in emptiness.

Two days later, after the Russian team had returned to Russia, he returned to Bangalore. At the airport, he saw his wife Vijayamma and Advocate Vijayakumar. Something unusual, especially the presence of Vijayakumar.

Am I going to be arrested at the airport. He wondered.

"Nothing so serious," Vijayakumar pacified him. "But we have to be careful."

On their way home, Vijayamma noticed two motorcycles following their car. She didn't know it was part of the surveillance. She didn't know her house had been under IB surveillance for more than three weeks. She didn't know their camera with loaded film and a video cassette, both carrying proof of the visit of the Glavkosmos team, had reached the hands of IB through her maidservant. She didn't know Mariam Rasheeda had named her husband as a member of the spy ring. She didn't know she couldn't get many of her relatives in Kerala on the phone because they had been threatened by the police. She didn't know the police was trying to plant proof in her house to establish that she was running a brothel.

Yes, the Deputy General Manager of HMT, a state-owned holding company of the Government of India, was oblivious of many things happening around her.

▼

The next day, 4 p.m.

A knock at the door woke up Chandrasekhar from his nap. Four men, whom he was seeing for the first time, and the SI of Hebba police station greeted him. A tall man with cropped hair and a thick moustache introduced himself as Siby Mathews, DIG and leader of the SIT investigating the ISRO espionage case. He introduced the team members – Babu Raj SP Joshua SP, and Vimal Kumar S.I.

"We want to search your house," Babu Raj told Chandrasekhar.

"Where's the warrant?" Chandrasekhar asked.

"Will reach you soon." Siby Mathews threw a smile at him. Before his smile faded, his eyes glowed. They fell on a model of PSLV on the table. Siby Mathews took it in his hands.

"Where did you get this from?" he asked.

"It was presented to me by Prof Marchuk."

"Who is that guy? Why did he give it to you?"

"Marchuk is one of the foreign consultants of ISRO. He was once the Vice-President of Russia."

"So that is how the Russian link goes," Siby Mathews was in a contemplative mood. Chandrasekhar didn't understand the pun Siby gave on 'link'. But he knew ISRO had invited Prof Marchuk to analyse the failure of the development launch of PSLV in 1993.

"So you keep a model of PSLV at home!" Siby Mathews went on.

"What is so great in it?" Chandrasekhar asked him. "This was originally presented to Prof Marchuk by Prof U.R. Rao, ISRO Chairman, along with a book he wrote. Marchuk presented me the same model after I signed a contract with Glavkosmos."

Siby Mathews cut him short through gesture. He didn't want any explanation from Chandrasekhar.

That was when Babu Raj came with a new model, quite different from what Siby Mathews was holding. He had unearthed it from the master bedroom.

"Here is one," Babu Raj was thrilled.

Chandrasekhar didn't clarify it was a model of VOSTOK, a Russian rocket.

Suddenly, the fax machine became operative. The search team rushed to his office room. A message from ISRO. Nay, it was a letter ISRO had sent to Aleksey V. Vasin, redirected to Chandrasekhar.

Siby Mathews took the fax message. His face turned red. IB had told him about Aleksey Vasin, the guy in Glavkosmos with whom Nambi Narayanan had struck a deal to transfer four bundles of the drawings of Viking technology; the middle-man to smuggle the documents to Pakistan.

Siby Mathews searched the fax file as a man possessed. He drew a few messages out.

"How did you intercept the secret message from ISRO?" Siby was in a grilling mood.

"I didn't intercept. The message might not have been clear. So the Glavkosmos people refaxed it to me to help ascertain from ISRO the content of the letter."

"But, why you?"

"I am their agent."

Siby Mathews felt he had struck gold. He heard what he wanted to hear.

Joshua prepared the search warrant. Among the evidence seized, he included the PSLV model which any Tom, Dick or Harry could purchase for a couple of hundred bucks from the ISRO headquarters.

For a moment, Chandrasekhar thought he was witnessing an absurd drama in which the investigating officials were idiots.

"You have to sign a couple of papers at the Hebba Police Station," Siby Mathews said before he escorted Chandrasekhar out.

It was twilight and Vijayamma was lighting the lamp in her pooja room when she heard Babu Raj saying, "You need not worry about your husband."

The next morning, she saw her husband at the airport. Advocate Vijayakumar had informed her the previous night that Chandrasekhar will have to go to Thiruvananthapuram to sign some papers. She gave him a briefcase with a few clothes for his short stay in Thiruvananthapuram. She also told him that his room had been reserved at Hotel South Park. Chandrasekhar gave his wife no hint that he was under arrest.

Siby Mathews had instructed him not to tell Vijayamma anything about the arrest. "In that case," he had cautioned Chandrasekhar, "we will have to arrest her also."

"Do you know your husband has been staying with Mariam Rasheeda for many years? He is cheating on you." Babu Raj came close to Vijayamma and asked as she was walking towards her car.

"I know my husband, the way your wife knows you. How would she react if similar things are told to her about you?" Vijayamma cut him short.

"Okay. Where can one get costly silk sarees from?" Babu Raj enquired with a smile.

"There is nothing so special in Bangalore which you can't get in Thiruvananthapuram," she said trying to avoid him.

"You people are enjoying life. You are a member of many clubs," Babu Raj said poking his head into the car.

"And what is wrong with that?" Vijayamma asked.

"Nothing, except that you shall never enter those clubs again."

Vijayamma felt the venom. She looked at Babu Raj, scared. But he had walked away. She decided to take a day's leave from the office. The venom had started to spread. She began to sweat, in and out. She heard her heartbeat, like someone clubbing her head in rhythmic succession.

What is happening to me? What is happening to my Chandra?

▼

Standing almost naked in a room in the guest house of Hindustan Latex in front of the interrogators, Chandrasekhar also didn't know what was happening to him. He only knew they were plucking his beard with pliers and raining blows on his face. They even cracked a joke that the blows won't leave any marks, thanks to his beard.

Then, he found himself standing inside the accused box in a courtroom. It was a two-minute affair. He thought it was all over. He decided not to tell Vijayamma anything about what had happened to him.

While returning from the court, the SI asked him to remove his wristwatch and wedding ring. "You are under arrest for doing espionage," the SI said.

He didn't understand its full implication. The low decibel voice of the SI sounded very familiar. But he couldn't locate the man behind the voice. He couldn't locate even himself.

"Even if my father is brought here," the SI continued, "he will have to repeat what we teach him to tell. Otherwise, we break his bones. Not only his bones, but his wife's and children's bones too. It is our unwritten law. You say what they ask you to say. Then you alone would suffer. Don't you love your family?"

The SI removed his cap and smiled. In the next moment, Chandrasekhar recalled the police officer. It was Thampi S. Durgadatt. He had seen the SI in mufti in the waiting room of Dr Girija, his cousin, when he had come for a heart checkup of Vijayamma. Thampi had come with his mother.

"Don't you remember me?" Chandrasekhar caught hold of the SI's hand and asked. "Do you think I am a spy?"

"Yes, I remember you. I am sorry I have to see you like this. Please tell the IB people what they want you to tell them. Don't you know the statements you give before the police have no value before the court?" Thampi smiled. Chandrasekhar felt at ease. For a moment he forgot his hands were cuffed.

He was brought back to the guest house of Hindustan Latex.

"Where do you stay while in Madras?" Mr B asked.

"Hotel Connemara or Chola."

"No. You have to tell a different story. You were staying in Madras International."

"I have never been to that hotel. You can verify my records."

"You have to say that you were In Madras International on 24 January." This time it was Mr A.

"Do you want me to tell lies?"

A blow on his face left Chandrasekhar bleeding.

"Behave properly. Repeat what we say. Learn them by heart. We know you are a liar. All other members of your gang have agreed that they met you at Madras International. Raman Srivastava has agreed. Sasikumaran has agreed. Fauziya Hassan has agreed. Mariam Rasheeda has agreed. Now, tell us, from where did you pick up Srivastava? Tell us what all documents were transacted in return for one lakh US dollars?"

Chandrasekhar looked at the three-member team in utter disbelief. Am I seeing things? Am I losing my mental balance? Who are these men staring at me? Will I ever see Vijayamma and my mother?

Oh! I have to attend her eighty-fourth birthday.

In the next moment, he heard two shrill cries, that of his wife and mother.

"Unless you tell the story, we shall torture your wife and mother. They are in the next room. Your mother can now celebrate your death. Or you can celebrate her death. If you are interested in seeing your wife being raped in front of you and your mother, we can even do it for you. We want to keep you spies in good humour." Mr A gave him a slap and asked, "How do you know S.K. Sharma?"

"We are friends."

"Why did Sharma take Fauziya and Mariam to the Army Club?"

"I don't know."

"Who is the Brigadier?"

"I don't know any Brigadier."

"Who is Wing Commander Sharma?"

"I don't know."

"Don't you know he is your friend Sharma's father-in-law?"

"I had met him. But I don't know his rank."

"So you know him. Similarly, you know Brigadier Srivastava also."

"I don't know any Srivastava."

Chandrasekhar felt a rude blow on his head. He swooned. Mr A then gave direction to his subordinate officer to switch the tape off. Chandrasekhar's mother and wife stopped crying.

When he woke up, he found Siby Mathews, Joshua and a new face talking to the three wise men of IB. Mr A was holding a copy of the *Mathrubhumi* newspaper. Its headline was "PSLV First Launch Failure Due To Sabotage".

Siby Mathews threw the paper on Chandrasekhar's face. He read the news:

> *There is clear information that the failure of the first launch of PSLV on 20 September 1993 was due to sabotage. The sabotage has caused a loss of over Rs 60 crores to ISRO and spoiled the efforts of thousands of scientists. It has also pulled India's space technology back. ISRO scientist D. Sasikumaran and Glavkosmos agent K. Chandrasekhar were the brains behind the sabotage.*

He couldn't read further. He felt dizzy. His throat became dry. He asked for a cup of water. Mr A told him they don't have time and he better answer their questions. The clock ticked 11. He watched the pendulum swinging and listened to the music of the bell when he noticed the date on the dial. 28 November!

"My mother, it is your birthday!" He started weeping.

Through the flowing veil of teardrops, he saw a woman entering the room. Mother? He wiped his eyes. It was Fauziya Hassan.

"Do you know him?" Siby Mathews asked the Maldivian woman.

"Yes."

"When did you meet him?"

"At Madras."

"What did he give you?"

"A cover."

"What did you give him in return?"

"One lakh American dollars."

That was a slap on his faith in human beings. 'Is this the same woman whom I had helped in her distress? How could she tell such a lie? And why should she?'

"What are you saying Fauziya? Have you gone mad?" Chandrasekhar interrupted.

"One lakh American dollars," she repeated.

"How big was the packet?" Chandrasekhar asked Fauziya.

"Two inches."

"How can you hold one lakh dollars in a two-inch packet, Fauziya?"

'Then it could be a bigger packet."

"In which hotel did we meet at?"

"I don't remember."

"Room number."

"Don't remember."

"Time?"

"I don't know."

Fauziya Hassan then looked at the wise men of IB. Mr A came to her help.

"Good Chandrasekhar, you are arguing like Advocate K.K. Venugopal. But sorry, this is not the court of justice."

It was followed by a powerful blow on his left ear. He didn't see who hit him. But he heard the voice of Mr B.

"We know how to make you tell the truth. Tomorrow your wife's photograph will appear in all newspapers. She is running a brothel in your house."

Something cracked inside. Chandrasekhar felt his chest breaking into pieces. He screamed.

"Bring a rope. Let's hang him head down," he heard Mr A thundering.

"I want to lie down. My heart is breaking," Chandrasekhar pleaded with folded hands.

"Lie on the floor, if you can't stand." Mr A showed kindness. Chandrasekhar groaned in pain. A black hefty doctor came rushing in.

"Take him to the hospital immediately," he heard the doctor saying.

▼

Something different happened at Bangalore around the same time.

Vijayamma had locked the house from inside. She had given strict direction to her security not to let anybody in. She was about to go to bed when she heard someone quarrelling on the road. She heard a woman screaming. In the dim light outside, she saw a woman fling the gate open. She heard continuous knocking at her door. The woman was crying aloud. She was pleading with Vijayamma to open the door and let her in.

Vijayamma came down from her bedroom and asked the woman to move close to the window so that she could see her. But the woman preferred not to show her face to Vijayamma. She felt something was fishy and told the woman she would not let her in. At the other end of the road, she saw a group of men watching the drama.

A few minutes later, the woman stopped crying and walked towards the gate and joined the group outside. And they disappeared into the dark.

Two minutes later, a police jeep slowed near her house and then sped away. Vijayamma got frightened. She opened the freezer and took out an ice cube. She rolled it on her forehead, fearing her head would break. She stretched her hand for the TV remote. She changed the channels to kill the night.

And then, a black screen.

The national channel!

25

Chocolates

14 January 1995

Armed policemen took control of the jail premises. Shooters stood ready at vantage points. Everything was ready. Everybody was ready. It was red alert in Viyyur Central Prison.

Any time a Pakistani helicopter could land in, break cell no 5, and free S.K. Sharma, the sixth accused in the ISRO espionage case. He was their man; the crucial link between ISI and some top brass in the Indian Army.

Sitting in cell 6, Nambi Narayanan watched a couple of gun-wielding policemen stationed in front of his cell. He saw the jail Superintendent walking briskly towards Sharma's cell.

"What's the problem?" Nambi Narayanan asked the Superintendent.

He said something which Nambi Narayanan didn't understand. He wanted to meet the jail doctor. Something was scratching inside his head. It was the doctor who told him about a sensational newspaper report.

A local newspaper, quoting highly placed sources in IB, had flashed the story that the ISI would "airlift Sharma today".

On his way back to the cell, Sukumaran, a man in his forties, approached Nambi Narayanan. Convicted for life, Sukumaran had three murders and two rapes to his credit.

"Can you sir," Sukumaran whispered. "Please, ask your friend to take me with him? I want to live. I love life."

Nambi Narayanan didn't know what to say. He nodded. He didn't agree or deny. But to Sukumaran, the nod signalled a positive cue. He smiled with an ocean of gratitude.

"Keep it a secret," he whispered. He then vanished to emerge once the helicopter landed.

"Why so many policemen?" Sharma couldn't resist asking Nambi Narayanan as he was coming close to his cell.

"To prevent the ISI from airlifting you."

"Who is ISI?" Sharma asked curiously.

Nambi Narayanan didn't say anything. He was witnessing the innocence of a simple human being labelled as a dreaded spy.

'Why didn't Nambi Narayanan answer me,' Sharma thought. Later, with pain in his heart, he realized that all his questions, since Chandrasekhar gave him a frantic phone call, had remained unanswered.

The call came on 21 October 1994 at his office in Vijaya Steel Lid. His friendship with Chandrasekhar began at the age of 24. Sharma then was a transport operator, and Chandrasekhar was doing some agency work.

"Do you know who this girl is?" Chandrasekhar asked from the other end.

"Which girl?" Sharma asked.

"Mariam Rasheeda."

"Who is that?"

"The young Maldivian woman."

It was Chandrasekhar who introduced Mariam Rasheeda and Fauziya Hassan to Sharma. He asked Sharma to help Fauziya Hassan get admission for her daughter in the Baldwin Girls High School. Thomas, the principal's husband, was Sharma's good friend.

Sharma picked the women, one an old lady and the other, a young one, from Cooks Town and drove his car towards the principal's house. On the way, he heard Fauziya Hassan crying. Somebody had cheated her by taking Rs 25,000 for the school admission.

"I can take you to Domlur Police Station. You better lodge a complaint," Sharma advised her.

"No," the old lady said. "What will I do if he troubles my daughter? She will have to be in Bangalore alone once I leave for the Maldives."

After meeting Thomas, Sharma asked them to take an auto-rickshaw and go to High Street, Cooks Town.

He met them again, the same evening, at the school. He had managed a seat for Fauziya's daughter. On their way back, Fauziya wanted to go to the loo, and Sharma drove the car to Ranjit Singh Institute, better known as the Army Club since retired Squadron Leader Bhasin, his father-in-law's friend, was also in the car. Bhasin was a member of the club.

"Mariam Rasheeda has been arrested by the Kerala Police," Chandrasekhar sounded worried at the other end.

"In what way am I connected?" Sharma asked.

"The news report says she is a spy," Chandrasekhar said.

"Spy!" Sharma couldn't believe it. "Damn it." He put the phone down without waiting for Chandrasekhar to disconnect the line.

A week later, Chandrasekhar gave another frantic call. He sounded nervous. Some IB officers had questioned him in connection with her arrest. After a few days, Chandrasekhar came to E.C.A. Club where Sharma was playing badminton. He looked happy and relieved of tension.

"They have cleared me. It was some wild suspicion."

Sharma too felt relieved. The friends sipped whiskey.

Nothing happened for two weeks until Sharma got a call from Vijayamma. The Deputy General Manager of Hindustan Machine Tools sounded shattered. Some police officers from Kerala, she told him, had taken her husband Chandrasekhar with them. They also searched her house. She didn't know where they had taken him. Nobody told her anything.

The next moment, Sharma's phone rang again. His wife Kiran told him that a police officer, S. Jogesh, had been to their house. He told her to inform her husband that the police wanted to meet him the next day at his office.

And they came. Siby Mathews, DIG; G. Babu Raj, SP; Jogesh, CI and a couple of local policemen.

"How do you know Chandrasekhar?" Siby Mathews asked.

"My friend," Sharma said.

"Since when?"

"From, say, 1978."

"OK! We want to search your office." Siby Mathews gave him a paper. It was the order of XI Additional Chief Metropolitan Magistrate, Bangalore, dated 21 November 1994. The order was issued to the Inspector of Police, Special Branch, CID, Thiruvananthapuram, Kerala State, to search his factory.

"Where is your office? Quick," Siby Mathews was on his heels.

"This." Sharma showed the room in which they were sitting.

"No. Your factory."

"I don't have one. I am a labour contractor. Vijaya Steels Ltd. has allotted me this small room in their premises."

The cops looked at each other in utter disbelief.

The search was conducted. In column 4 of the search list, where you describe the articles found during the search, Inspector Jogesh wrote, NIL.

The team wanted to see his house. And before that, the Army Club.

"I am not a member. Let me try uncle Bhasin," Sharma gave him a ring. In less than thirty minutes, the retired Squadron Leader was in front of Vijaya Steels.

At the Army Club, Bhasin offered the cops tea. But they were on duty and refused to accept free peas.

"Do you know Mariam Rasheeda?" Siby Mathews came to the point.

"You mean the Maldivian woman? I don't know who among the two women is Mariam Rasheeda. But I had taken them here a few months back."

Siby Mathews then scanned the Club records.

"OK! Now we are going to your house, Sharma," Siby Mathews rose from his seat.

"Nothing to be worried," Babu Raj told Sharma when he asked why there were police vans in front of his house. When they entered the house, Jogesh gave him another search warrant.

"This one to search the house."

After another forty-five minutes of search, Jogesh entered NIL against column 4. Again.

"Sorry, Mr Sharma. But you see, it is our job," Siby Mathews sounded a bit apologetic. Sharma just stared at them.

The next morning, a call from Siby Mathews made him stare at the whole world.

"You are hiding a lot of things, Sharma. You have to come to Thiruvananthapuram. Our higher officials from Delhi have to question you. Be there on the 27th. At your own expense."

27 November was a Sunday. So Sharma left Bangalore one day early. He took with him Raju, a friend, and Tomy Sebastian, a

Bangalore-based Malayalee lawyer, hoping that he would be of great help to Chandrasekhar in getting bail.

They checked into Rooms 310 and 314 at Hotel Pankaj, opposite the State Secretariat. Before he had ordered anything, Tomy Sebastin traced the phone number of Siby Mathews. The DIG was not there. Sharma informed the constable about his stay in Thiruvananthapuram. Two hours later at 3:30 p.m., his phone rang.

"Nice that you have come. We will meet tomorrow." It was Babu Raj, SP.

"Why can't we make it today itself?" Sharma asked.

"Not possible. We are awaiting officers from Delhi," Babu Raj cut the line.

The waiting continued for four more days. Meanwhile, Raju returned to Bangalore, and Sharma and his advocate moved to Room 315.

The next day, he got a frantic call from his wife Kiran. "Where have you gone, man? Absconded? Siby Mathews has just phoned me and said that you have absconded."

"Where can I go?" Sharma shouted at her. "Don't you know I had never been to Thiruvananthapuram before? Again, is it not you who contacted me?" Sharma couldn't understand why the police officer should tell a lie. He became a bit agitated. He dialled Siby Mathews. At the other end, it was again Babu Raj.

"Okay. You are still there? We have been told that you have vacated rooms 310 and 314. So we thought you might have absconded."

"And you didn't bother to check whether I have moved to some other room in the same hotel? The change has been recorded in the register. Don't you know I have come here at my expense and have been waiting for the last five days for you people to question me? Why should you scare my wife? This is cruel." Sharma didn't wait for the reply. He banged the phone. He didn't know the cruel part was yet to come.

On 1 December, Babu Raj came to his room around 1:30 p.m. There were a couple of policemen with him. They took Sharma to the Cantonment Police Station and left him there. His advocate was not permitted in, nor was he given food at the station.

The next day, around 2 p.m. Jogesh came rushing to the station. "Quick. We have to move," he said. He didn't ask whether Sharma had been given any food since he was taken under custody.

After an hour or so, Sharma found himself standing in the accused box in the court of Additional Chief Judicial Magistrate. The Magistrate glanced through the Remand Report submitted by K.K. Joshua, Narcotic Cell SP. Para 4 and 5 of the report read:

> *During the investigation, I got information that S.K. Sharma has moved out of Bangalore with an advocate and was staying in Hotel Pankaj, Thiruvananthapuram. I arrested him from a place near the hotel and kept him under custody in Cantonment Police Station. The arrest was informed to advocate Tomy Sebastian, who had accompanied him from Bangalore. On questioning, the accused has pleaded guilty.*

Sharma heard the magistrate pronounce the order. "Remanded to police custody till 12 December..."

He stood shell-shocked.

"I have never done any crime. I am only a friend of Chandrasekhar. I came here because DIG Siby Mathews had asked me to come over to Thiruvananthapuram. You are linking my name to ISRO. I don't know its full form. Show me at least one person in the whole of ISRO who knows me personally. It is a mistake. I am not a spy," Sharma said.

The Magistrate tossed the remand report and the Bench clerk called the next case number. A constable pushed Sharma out of the accused box.

The court is busy. Justice has to be delivered. Only Sharma didn't know that.

Next day, *Desabhimani*, the Marxist newspaper, reported:

The Special Investigation Team has arrested yet another top rung scientist of the ISRO spy ring. S.K. Sharma, a former scientist with the ISRO, is now with the Defence Research and Development Laboratory. It is believed S.K. Sharma has played a significant role in leaking sensitive information about missile technology to enemy countries. DRDL is the nerve centre of missile technology-related research works.

Kerala Kaumudi reported:

The police raided Sharma's house and office in Bangalore and have seized many incriminating documents. Chandrasekhar and Sharma are business partners importing components for space and defence research. They have been spying on documents through their business. The police have seized tell-tale documents.

▼

S.K. Sharma, forty-one years, holder of an Arts Degree, who began his career as a transport company manager, didn't see the pieces of investigative journalism. Nobody bothered to translate the stories into English, Hindi or Kannada.

'Why did it happen to me?' Sitting in his cell, Sharma soliloquized. He was trying to forget everything.

But how could he forget the evening of 7 January 1995?

Sharma, like the other accused, hoped he would get bail from the CBI court. The CJM court had already granted them bail. His wife Kiran had come from Bangalore to take him back. She was sitting in the front row in the courtroom. He threw a broken smile at her. She waved her hands, signalling victory.

But the CBI court denied him bail. He didn't dare to look at Kiran. He didn't want to break down in front of her.

At 5 p.m. he had three visitors – Kiran, his daughter, and his father-in-law. The child couldn't recognize him. He had a beard and he was in his jail dhoti. He didn't want her to recognize him, either. Kiran gave a packet to the superintendent. He opened the small brown packet and gave it to Sharma.

Chocolates!

Sharma couldn't control himself. He broke down. Kiran pressed her child closer to her heart.

"Give one or two to your daughter. Don't you know she likes chocolates more than her toys? But, she has stopped eating chocolates. I can't stand this anymore. I want to see her tasting chocolates again. Please." Kiran held her breath for a while.

Sharma took a handful of chocolates. He opened his daughter's fist and filled it with red, blue, green and yellow chocolates. He kissed her forehead.

The child got the smell of her father. She stared at his bearded face. The child saw her father. She smiled.

She looked at the chocolates in her hands. She smiled.

But she couldn't understand why all the others around her were weeping.

Night fell. Sharma fell asleep, unable to bear the pangs of life.

In his cell, Sukumaran, a convicted criminal who had three murders and two rapes to his credit was waiting for the helicopter to come.

26

Cries and Whispers

6 September 1997

Court of the Sessions Judge, Thiruvananthapuram.

Judge M.A. Nissar passed his orders in a Criminal Miscellaneous Petition.

"The offences alleged against the petitioner are bailable. The maximum punishment for the said offences is imprisonment for a period of two years. The petitioner has been in custody for more than two years. Therefore, it is a fit case to grant bail to the petitioner on self-bond as, even if she jumps bail, she has already suffered more than the prescribed sentence for the offence."

The petitioner Mariam Rasheeda, under trial, R.P. 431, Viyyur Central Prison, Kerala saw a flicker of hope. The bail was in two separate defamation cases filed by Circle Inspector Vijayan against her for daring to tell *India Today* that the interrogators had tortured her and to confide to *Savvy* magazine that she was implicated in a false case for having spurned of the sexual advances of a police officer.

Earlier, she was discharged in the espionage case and the corruption case. Besides, the court had acquitted her in the overstay case. Now, with bail granted in the pending defamation cases, Mariam heaved a sigh of relief. Still, she was apprehensive. She saw how the government had invoked NSA against Fauziya Hassan the moment she was discharged from all cases against her.

Mariam raised her apprehension before the court. Judge M.A. Nissar passed another order the same day. "The Public Prosecutor submits that there is no case against the petitioner and the petitioner's apprehension of arrest is unreal. In view of this submission, the Crl. M.C. No. 1538/97 is closed."

The evening was usually cool and calm. But the sky was cloudy. For the first time in three years, Mariam Rasheeda felt the 312 km journey back to prison by road inspiring that she didn't see the gathering storm.

She was looking inside and listened to the whispers of her ruptured soul. She closed her eyes. The caravan of memories drowned her in a deluge of images.

▼

1994. Love at first sight.

Dr Anand David Saldhana, Asst. Professor, Medical College, Mangalore, reminded Mariam Rasheeda of her lost boyfriend.

A week later, Dr Anand got a letter from Mariam Rasheeda sent to his home address. She wanted to meet him once again at her host's house in Bangalore.

Four days later, he got another letter. She was to leave for Thiruvananthapuram the same day. Anand went to Bangalore, but the train had departed. In the letter, she had given the phone number of Hotel Samrat for him to contact her. After two marriages and two divorces, Mariam Rasheeda somehow felt this man would prove to be her Mr Right.

At the hotel, she waited for his calls. But he didn't call her.

She tried him on his phone several times. She wanted him to come to Kerala. Finally, when he came, the two met at the Kozhikode railway retiring room and exchanged hearts.

She was to leave for the Maldives on 29 September 1994 and her name had figured in the PNR manifest of the Indian Airlines flight to the Maldives. But the plane left without her because she couldn't get a cab to reach the airport. A national *bandh* by the Left parties against India signing the General Agreement on Tariffs and Trade (GATT) blocked her journey to the Maldives.

She postponed her journey by a week. But this time also, she couldn't make it since the biological warfare the CIA had tested on Indian soil had taken the subcontinent to a plague scare, and flights from India were cancelled from 4 October. And she was not sure whether she could return before 17 October, the date on which her permitted stay in India would end.

The best option was to get a NOC from the Police Commissioner for a stay beyond 17. On 8 October, she, accompanied by Fauziya Hassan, went to the Foreigners' Section in the Commissioner's office where she met Circle Inspector Vijayan, the man who wrecked her life. After taking her air tickets to the Maldives, he asked her to come after two days.

She did so, but he was not there.

The third day, Inspector Vijayan came to meet her in Room 205 in Hotel Samrat. He asked Fauziya Hassan to wait outside. He then touched her with unsavoury intentions. True, Mariam Rasheeda has no great regard for the Victorian morality. She had freaked out and flirted with many. But she didn't like the bull-like Vijayan. She didn't like the way he touched her. She couldn't stand his palpable lust.

"*Bas*..." she yelled. "Get out!"

Eight days later, Inspector Vijayan arrested her for overstaying and paved the way for IB to plant an espionage story.

Then it was hell.

Interrogators beat her black and blue. They stripped her naked and forced her to stand without sleep for nights together.

Mr A fondled her breasts. "It still sells," he said.

He took pliers in his hands. Mariam Rasheeda didn't see that. She was looking at his face. Suddenly she felt her genitals being torn.

The needle nose pliers in Mr A's hand had a tuft of her pubic hair. He threw it on her face.

"Put a crab in her crotch," he said to Vijayan.

▼

"Let's have tea," the woman constable who had been with Mariam Rasheeda during most of her journeys from the prison to courts and back, said. The driver too needed a small break.

Mariam Rasheeda rose from her seat. Her right knee suddenly ached badly. It had been so for a long time. She caressed the lump, the size of a cricket ball; the mark of the blow the wise men of IB gave her to identify the photo of Raman Srivastava.

It had been the sixth day of interrogation. Inspector Vijayan brought a couple of photographs and handed them over to Mr B.

"We don't want you," Mr A showed the photograph of a policeman in uniform. "We want only our people. We shall let you free if you would tell before the video that you know this officer and that he had taken you and Fauziya to the Army Club in Bangalore."

Mariam Rasheeda was seeing the man in the photo for the first time. "He is not that man. He is different. Who is this? I haven't seen him."

"He is Brigadier Srivastava who had taken you to the Army Club." Mr A was assertive. "Nice girl. All you have to do is to identify his photographs. You will be a free bird the next moment."

"But tell me why am I here? Is it because I asked your inspector to get out? You have stripped me naked, denied me food and sleep, and molested me. What for? Why should I trust you now? I don't believe you suckers..."

She wanted to say something more. Instead, she cried aloud with excruciating pain. Mr A had given her a rude blow, below her right knee, with a rod.

"Bring her mother and daughter. Let them see her in nude before we rape them in front of her," Mr A declared his manifesto.

Mariam Rasheeda succumbed to the physical and mental torture. She 'identified' the photograph as that of Raman Srivastava IG, the kingpin of the spy ring, of which she was the queen bee.

The gripping pain was still there. The swell had turned to a lump. At times it ached badly.

"Can you please bring my tea here?" she requested the woman constable. "My leg is giving me problems."

Sipping the hot tea, Mariam Rasheeda told the friendly woman constable: "I am free. I never thought I could come out of this prison. I should be thankful to the Indian judiciary. Now I can see my daughter and my mother. I have some health problems. In fact, I came to India for treatment. This lump is causing me serious problem. But I won't treat it. Let it continue to pain my body and mind till I take my last breath. It is my repentance for having dragged the name of your IG, a man I had never seen, to the spy case. But then, I had no other option."

The pain grew. The pain submerged her in its spell. And she fell asleep.

The woman constable woke her up. She was back in the prison. Tomorrow, she thought, or the day after tomorrow, I can fly back to the Maldives.

The warden gave her two packets. One white and the other, brown. She opened the brown. She read it, screamed aloud, and swooned.

Mariam Rasheeda felt she was inside a fluid tunnel. Fauziya was sitting beside her. She gave the paper to Fauziya, three years older than her mother. Fauziya caught hold of her hands, hugged her. While reading Mariam's detention order under NSA for one year, she felt Mariam's teardrops falling on her breast.

Fauziya then opened the white cover.

Dear Mother,

How are you? I am fine. I have a friend here. When you send the next letter, please mother, tell me the day you return. I shall wait for you at the airport. How is your illness? When will you be discharged from the hospital?

I am sad, mother, I am sad. I don't know when you would return. Please, come soon. I want to see you. I love you. Good luck, mother!

Your Nasiha

27

Baptism

1 April 1998

Every year, on this day, you allow yourself to be fooled by anyone. A funny ritual to make you believe you get fooled only once in a year!

Inside the court room of the Supreme Court of India, where the air was cool, D. Sasikumaran, 53 years, Scientist-G, ISRO, felt hot. He unbuttoned the top half of his white half-sleeve shirt.

His trauma began in a clumsy Magistrate's court in Thiruvananthapuram on 21 November 1994 after the police arrested him on charges of espionage. The courtroom was a pre-historic space with barricades raised here and there. The Magistrate, whose face he doesn't remember and a herd of advocates, whose faces he didn't see at all, sat face to face to deliver justice. The room was predominantly black. Black cloaks were flowing, standing or sitting.

Why justice should need this much of black to surface, he wondered.

The magistrate was not holding a hammer. But his words, "remanded to police custody" had an in-built hammer.

The first sting. The first drop of water. The first lick of fire.

The grinding had begun. The madness was to follow.

When did it begin?

After he received a phone call from Chandrasekhar, agent of Glavkosmos, to get the phone number of Hotel Samrat in Thiruvananthapuram?

Or when he took Mariam Rasheeda for dinner?

Or when *Desabhimani* hinted that he was a spy?

Or when ISRO transferred him to Ahmedabad?

Or when he was arrested?

The technocrat, who would have become a top brass in the Steel Authority of India, had he not joined ISRO in 1970, couldn't pinpoint the beginning of his trauma. He only knew the master fabricator, featured on print when Rohini began orbiting the earth in 1980, is now being featured as a spy, traitor, womanizer, et al.

Sasikumaran was in Kodaikanal with his wife, Dr Sarojaya, who was leading a group of medical students on a study tour. They were enjoying the beauty of nature when the news of Mariam Rasheeda's arrest reached him. He never thought she, who could hardly speak a complete sentence in English and mistook him as a doctor, could ever be a spy.

But the hint in the story that he was a member of the spy ring came as a rude shock. He shot off a letter to the ISRO Chairman, explaining his innocence. But ISRO management didn't take it at its face value. The administration shot an unwarranted letter to police demanding more details about the alleged crime.

Some self-claimed patriots pelted stones at his house.

Meanwhile, Sen Gupta, IAS, Joint Secretary, Department of Space, showed undue interest in the case and transferred him from the Liquid Propulsion Systems Centre to Space Application Centre, Ahmedabad, giving the impression that there was something rotten in ISRO. Few knew Sen Gupta was taking vengeance on D. Sasikumaran.

Two weeks after he joined Ahmedabad in shame and humiliation, the police brought him back under arrest.

Dr Sarojaya swooned.

The next day, a photo of her husband was on the front page of all newspapers, branded a spy.

▼

Hitting hard on your ears is more painful than branding you a spy; at least for those few seconds following the bolt. There was an explosion inside his head and blood started oozing out. Slowly, Sasikumaran realised his ears had lost their sharpness.

The IB sleuths asked him to name S. Nambi Narayanan. He did. They asked him to implicate Raman Srivastava. He did. He did everything he was asked to do in front of the video camera. Every time, he believed the truth would triumph. But every time, his trust in the system ditched him.

The CBI interrogators were as cruel as the IB men. He wondered how his body and mind could stand this much torture.

While investigating his 'spy background', CBI found his wealth was disproportionate to his known sources of income. They filed a case against him with the co-accused in the spy case as abettors.

▼

After days of torture, it was an era of leisure.

The cell in Viyyur Central Prison at Thrissur looked like a mansion compared to the small cubicle in Ernakulam sub-jail. It was during his leisurely life in Viyyur that Sasikumaran read *Kayar*, the masterpiece of Jnanpith recipient Thakazhi Sivasankara Pillai. He would not have dared to undertake that venture (the book had nearly a thousand pages!) but for his absolute leisure in the cell.

When he came out on bail after sixty days, he had put on four kilos.

▼

Original Petition, argument, counter, Writ Appeal, affidavit, rejoinder, exhibit, witness, cross-examination, trial, summary trial, chief examination, accused, acquittal, conviction, bail, anticipatory bail, stay, discharge...

What do they all mean? Every word has to be used carefully, more carefully than you fabricate a launcher. Once launched, they dart faster than your 338 tonnes GSLV, reach the orbit smoother and beam the signals clearer. More importantly, every word has an in-built bomb and a detonator.

It was what he was told when the legal process began. But nobody gave him a hint that the legal process would continue to be operative in one way or other even after the court would pass its final orders.

So, on 2 May 1996, when the CJM's court in Ernakulam discharged all the accused in the espionage case after the Magistrate was convinced that the charges were "false and baseless", D. Sasikumaran, the third accused, heaved a sigh of relief.

But it was for a flicker of a second. Inspector Vijayan moved a Criminal Revision Petition before Kerala High Court, praying that he be declared as the first informant in the spy case and given a fair chance to reopen the discharged case.

A week later, political power in Kerala changed in favour of the Marxists, who, by that time had declared that all institutions in India, except their comrades, IB, and Inspector Vijayan were unpatriotic.

So, the new Left government issued a notification for further investigation into the espionage case, even when the law of the land says that the State government has no authority under the IOS Act 1923 even to launch a complaint before a Magistrate in a case related to a Central government institution.

With the further investigation notification, the accused had to change their roles. He, along with the other discharged persons, became a complainant by challenging the government notification through writ petitions.

Meanwhile, the BJP and the CPI (M), through their political outfits, filed separate Criminal Revision Petitions before the High

Court, challenging the CJM order discharging all the accused in the espionage case. The technocrat-turned-complainant then became a counter petitioner.

After four months of arguments, the High Court dismissed all the Revision Petitions declaring that Inspector Vijayan and other public-spirited litigants had no *locus standi*.

The court also dismissed the petition of the accused in the further investigation case, but held that the Kerala government had no legal right to investigate the espionage case.

However, the CJM, Thiruvananthapuram gave formal permission to the Kerala Police to further investigate the case. Sasikumaran's name appeared again in the accused column. Back to square one.

The technocrat didn't want to go through the police mill once again. So he opted for the legal mill. He appealed to the High Court against the CJM order. Once again, the accused became a complainant.

Meanwhile, his friends had moved Special Leave Petitions (SLP) before the Supreme Court, challenging the High Court order. He went to Delhi to move his SLP, since by that time, he had lost faith in advocates. He had hired the best lawyers to fight his case. But he found them neither studying nor presenting the case properly. He read the relevant acts and soon got convinced that most of the advocates of this country didn't understand the Sections in the Acts properly.

He tried to educate even the Supreme Court lawyers, but they tossed away his treatises on law. Some even wondered whether the trauma had turned the technocrat abnormal. He wanted to educate the whole legal community, but they asked him to stick to rocket fabrication, and not law.

And, today, on the April Fool Day in 1996, he was going to argue his case himself; that too in the Supreme Court. He was nervous and stressed up. He sweated inside the courtroom of the Supreme Court of India, where the air was cool.

Yet, when his turn came, he rose and argued. After his argument was complete, he felt confident that he had presented his case well.

But not every other person! Out from the court, M.L. Sharma, Joint Director of CBI, came to him and said, "Sasi, you have made an ass of yourself."

He didn't answer. Many, including CBI, Sasi felt, had made him an ass.

'Now let me make myself an ass. There is at least some pleasure in it,' he soliloquized.

Walking towards the exit, he saw a queer thing. Siby Mathews, IG, was throwing away tea and biscuits offered by T.P. Senkumar DIG. That too inside the premises of the Supreme Court!

Back to the hotel in a taxi, Nambi Narayanan was sitting by his side. Nambi didn't say anything. He was looking outside, seeing nothing.

The car negotiated a curve. A two-storeyed building painted pistachio green, and an Alsatian in the portico pulled Sasikumaran's memories back to the days of ceaseless torture.

▼

There was silence in the building. It was the silence of twilight. The world had turned sepia. Sasikumaran was being escorted through a corridor. His figure was in silhouette. His hands were cuffed. A long chain from it was in the hand of an interrogator. He walked like a dog, on two legs. He sniffed blood. He was in front of a room with its door half-open. He turned his face to the left. A man was lying on the bench. His legs were swollen. They were bleeding. There were rashes on his body. He was groaning in pain. Sasikumaran couldn't see his face. But he knew who the wriggling soul was – the Princetonian! Dr Vikram Sarabhai's blue-eyed boy.

Sasikumaran felt pain in his ears.

'When did I first meet him?' he wondered. By a strange coincidence, Nambi Narayanan was also asking the same question to himself.

Sometime in the 1970s, Nambi Narayanan found an Ambassador car not giving way for his Lambretta scooter. The Kochuveli road was like a ribbon and it was difficult to overtake unless the man in front showed the traffic courtesy. Nambi Narayanan couldn't get a glimpse of the discourteous man till he managed to overtake the car. He stopped his scooter in front of the car and showered four-letter words on the man at the steering wheel. But all his abuses were returned in the same coin.

That afternoon, there was a conference. The Chairman ISRO had made Nambi Narayanan the one-man committee to study the points raised in the committee. A week later, when another committee deliberated his report, he saw the man with no traffic sense sitting opposite him. He felt a bit irritated. Maybe it was the reason why when he raised certain objections, Nambi Narayanan cut them short as a bunch of technical lies.

Sasikumaran looked at Nambi Narayanan. From that room in that two-storeyed building, Sasikumaran heard the groan again. Again and again.

He couldn't control his emotions. He caught hold of Nambi Narayanan's right hand. He held it tight. He pulled it towards his chest and fixed it close to his heart as if he wanted Nambi Narayanan to feel his heart.

He felt a palm caressing his bleeding heart instead.

Nambi Narayanan looked at him and saw the fabrication engineer crying like a dam with shutters full open.

28

The Fear of Freedom

30 November 1997

Fauziya Hassan, 54 years, a 5ft. tall frail woman and detenue no 199 of Viyyur Central Prison, was reading the weekly forecast in *The Indian Express* sitting in her cell. She had been reading it since she was labelled a spy. For reasons unknown to her, she jotted down the forecast in her notebook:

> *A series of extraordinary events will make the next week somewhat more lively than anticipated. If you are in tune with the mood of the moment, you will get the best out of opportunities and find a more appropriate solution to every problem. It is not a question of right or wrong, but of what works best.*

She closed the notebook, numbered twelve; her memoirs.

It was the end of a sunny day. Beams of sunlight fell slanting into her cell. At the other end of the cell, Mariam Rasheeda was scanning the glossy pages of the August '96 issue of *Companion*, a British magazine, sent to her by their one-time inmate in the cell, Samanta Slater, a British model for Coca Cola. The cover had the lusty face of David Woolley and it screamed in fluorescent rose letters, *Hello Boys: The Bad Girl's Guide to Good Sex.*

'Is Mariam reading a story on her?' Fauziya Hassan soliloquized with a smile.

Fauziya Hassan closed her eyes. In the dead vision inside her closed eyelids, she saw a cute face emerging through the pink dim light of her inner eyes. Her little Zila! She also saw the sprawling beaches of the Maldives and her lone son doing carpentry. She saw the dew-like face of her granddaughter, whose face she was yet to see.

And then, she saw the face she couldn't recognize - her own.

An expert tailor and a matriculate, Fauziya Hassan was with the Maldives Customs for four years. Married twice and divorced, she has a son and two daughters. In 1990, she moved to Sri Lanka with her little Zila, her youngest daughter through her second marriage.

Four years later, on 24 January, she came to India, her first visit to the country that ravished her. It was a kind of paid job to accompany two heart patients. Four months later, she came to India, seeking admission for Zila at Baldwin Girls High School, Bangalore.

After eleven days of stay in a hotel, she moved to the house of All Nasir, son of Ibrahim Nasir, the former President of Maldives, and from there to G-1 No-6/2, Auckland Residency, High Streets, Cooks Town, Bangalore, as paying guest of Sara Palani from where Kerala Police picked her, kept her under illegal detention for two days, and made her the first accused in the ISRO espionage case.

Three years had passed since. All the co-accused, except she and Mariam Rasheeda, were free. They had no money for security. Nobody to voice against their continued detention. Not even their country.

Fauziya Hassan had tempered her mind and body to reconcile herself to the reality that she was destined to end up in a cell.

It was then that the weekly fortune gave her a ray of hope. Only a ray.

The rest was darkness. The future, the present, the past!

▼

Now Fauziya Hassan was in the Hindustan Latex Guest House. End of a day's torture, she couldn't understand the story the interrogators were forcing her to repeat. She hadn't met Nambi Narayanan. She hadn't met Raman Srivastava. She knew Sasikumaran as a friend of Mariam Rasheeda. She knew S.K. Sharma, the stout man who seldom smiled. It was he who managed admission for her little Zila.

But the interrogators wanted her to tell something different. They had promised that she would be made an approver and would let her free if she would tell their version as her version in front of the video camera.

She had to say that she had been spying for Pakistan; had given Nambi Narayanan one lakh American dollars in exchange of documents and drawings of rockets; Zuheira, her friend, was a spy; Raman Srivastava IG was an active member of the spy ring, and that he was the same Brigadier Srivastava who took Mariam and her to the Army Club.

"What do you say?" Mr B asked her.

'What if I fall prey to these lies,' she thought, and said, "Sorry, I can't tell these lies."

Mr A came close to her, raised her face by her chin and slapped her. Not the first. "Let's waste no time. Let's bring her here. Let's rape her one by one in front of this old bitch," Mr A said.

Mr B nodded, yes.

"Who?" Fauziya asked.

"Zila." Mr A gave a frightening smile.

My thirteen-year-old girl! Allah! What sort of a trial is this? She felt dizzy. She saw little Zila standing in front of her, nude. She saw them ravishing her in succession. She saw blood streaming from her crotch. She heard Zila groaning in pain.

"No, no. Don't do it to my kid," Fauziya cried aloud. "Tell me what you want me to say."

Fauziya became a lamb. To save her lamb.

But halfway through the 'confession' she again cried aloud. "All lies. All lies. Can you ever prove these lies? Why did you threaten me that you will rape my little Zila?"

The video camera stopped whirling. Mr A came close to her. Another slap. She was thrown off balance. Her reading glass slipped off from her hand.

"We can make evidence. We can bribe people to appear as witnesses. You complete the recording, or we will throw you into the sea, alive. Nobody will ever know how you died. Nobody in India will question us. Better obey us. "

"When can I go?" Fauziya asked Mr A after she completed the recording. "I have said everything you have asked me to say. Allow me to go to my Zila. We shall leave India tomorrow. We shall never return."

Mr A didn't answer. He threw a smile at her. It took more than ten days for her to understand the meaning of that smile.

Mr A took her to a room. There she saw Chandrasekhar. He looked like a beggar in torn clothes. His face was swollen. He was crying like a baby.

"Ask him the questions as we have told you," Mr A whispered into her ears.

Am I trapping the man who helped me? But then, what's wrong in it if that can help me go free? Let me not be concerned about others. I alone can help my little Zila.

Yes, I am ready for the betrayal.

▼

Fauziya took a deep breath. The notebook was still in her hand. Mariam Rasheeda was still in her old position. Then she heard Mariam crying. She went up to her cellmate. Mariam was in deep sleep. Rivers of tears streamed down her cheeks. Fauziya wiped her face clean with the lace of her skirt. For a moment she thought it was her Zila. She caressed Mariam's forehead. Sleep my little child, sleep. It is a blessing.

▼

10 December 1997

Fauziya Hassan was taking her bath when a guard told her she was free. She couldn't believe the guard even though she had been expecting that news. She couldn't share the happiness with Mariam Rasheeda whom the jail authorities had taken to Thiruvananthapuram in connection with two separate defamation cases.

"Once again Fauziya, you are free," the jailor told her.

Once again, for the third time!

First, the CBI court discharged her from the last case pending against her in June 1996. It was the one registered under the Prevention of Corruption Act. The CJM court had already discharged her in the espionage case. She could have left for the Maldives the same day as there was no case pending against her. But the court ordered that her release was conditional. She didn't understand how a release could be conditional when there was no case against her in any courts in India. She collapsed in the accused box.

Within hours, Inspector Vijayan slammed a defamation case against her for an interview she had given to Asianet TV. Since there was nobody to take her on bail, Fauziya Hassan had to return to the same cell.

The second release was on 11 December 1996.

On that day, the Magistrate discharged her from the defamation case. Once again, she was free and could have left for the Maldives. But the government clamped an undeclared emergency on her by invoking the NSA. The detention was for one year.

After one year, she was now free. Once again!

Before Fauziya Hassan left the prison, a few inmates gave her some chocolates. She tasted one. She gave the jailer one, the warden one, and one each to the policemen who used to accompany her to different courts during the past three years.

She kept one chocolate, a bar of slab with blue and gold stripe wrapper, safe inside her purse. For her little Zila.

From the prison, she was escorted to the office of the Police Commissioner of Ernakulam. He formally informed her she was free and could go anywhere. He allowed her to make an international call to the Maldives using his office phone. But she did not remember her residence number. Somehow, her cousin's number flashed through her mind. She rang her, and through the cousin, got her phone number.

She heard the voice she had missed so long. Nasiha. She couldn't say anything. She just cried. It was suffering. End of suffering.

That night, she was taken to a convent. She couldn't sleep. She feared the excitement would end the next morning.

The next morning, a police constable came to the convent and asked Fauziya Hassan to meet the Commissioner. She thought her worst fears were going to come true and that she would be arrested again. The constable put her in a three-wheeler and asked the driver to take her to the Commissioner's office.

"How can I go alone?" she asked.

"You are free," he told her.

As the three-wheeler started moving, Fauziya Hassan realized she was free. But the fear of freedom gripped her. Three years of consternation had made her fear freedom. She held the auto-rickshaw driver's shoulders, shivering with fear.

At the Commissioner's office, Fauziya Hassan made a strange request.

"I want police protection."

Part - VII

Counter Narrative

29

Lies and Contrived Truths

The ISRO spy case is dead. And yet, not dead.

The case that appears to be a single case is a multi-layered and complex federation of mini-narratives in which timing of intersections, concinnity of melodramas, entry of the dramatis personae, and their eloquent silences were so neatly trimmed, timed, and fused that they unfolded like a single end to end espionage story.

So, there is the CIA that had been waiting for the opportune moment to derail India's cryogenic dreams by hook or crook; an Inspector of Kerala Police who wanted to save his skin that he painted a semi-literate Maldivian woman as the spy who had come to destabilize India's defence organizations; a newspaper Editor who wanted to take revenge on an arrogant politician and his blue-eyed IPS officer; a few top-level CIA moles in IB who planted what the CIA had fabricated; some top-ranking police officers of Kerala Police, including the DGP and a DIG, acting under the dictation of IB, thanks to its extra-constitutional authority nobody dares to question; the media-savvy Antony group in Kerala unit of the Congress Party and its unscrupulous group managers who wanted to do away with one of Kerala's most popular leaders so that its idealist leader could occupy the Chief Minister's chair; and the gluttony media that regurgitated the rotten feeds fed to them by the police and the politicians at regular intervals.

It is difficult to see through the opaque and intriguing layers that make the espionage story. CBI that investigated the case for 18 months, a judiciary that heard the case many times at many levels over a period of twenty-seven years, and a media that still regurgitate what is being fed to them without ever bothering to do a logical, intelligent and independent exploration of the whole episode – all have jointly blindfolded people with misinformation, disinformation and distorted information.

It is in this context one has to view the contours of a counter-narrative being worked out to project the ISRO espionage case as the sad story of an innocent victim; camouflaging the hidden agenda with wrong orbits, misleading trajectories, hoax fuels and leaky tanks veneered with a glossy coat of pseudo patriotism.

Interestingly, the man who scripts the counter-narrative is S. Nambi Narayanan, the old whipping boy of the media. He is doing it through selective use of the judicial system and a cleverly executed media explosion.

The Legal Jugglery

Let us see how Nambi Narayanan used the judicial system to benefit only him, keeping the other victims and the real facts behind the espionage case beyond the scope of legal interference.

On 3 June 1996, CBI filed a confidential report to Kerala government detailing certain "serious lapses" on the part of the SIT members of the Kerala Police, and demanded action against the erring police officers.

Though the DGP and the Chief Secretary opined no action was to be initiated against the police officers, the then Chief Minister E.K. Nayanar noted on 12 December 1996 that the final decision could wait till the Supreme Court's decision on the legality of the State government's order to further investigate the espionage case.

The Supreme Court quashed the Kerala government's order to further investigate as "patently invalid" on 29 April 1998. But E.K. Nayanar and three chief ministers who succeeded him slept over the file for over a dozen years.

On 29 June 2016, the Kerala government headed by Oommen Chandy, who had masterminded the political coup to oust K. Karunakaran as Chief Minister using the espionage case decided that no action was necessary against the members of SIT. (He did it to dispense with the implications of a PIL that I had filed before Kerala High Court in 2010.)

At this juncture, Nambi Narayanan approached the High Court seeking compensation for him and for taking actions against the Kerala Police officers, which was finally settled in his favour by the Supreme Court on 14 September 2018.

The court awarded fifty lakh rupees as compensation for Nambi Narayanan and constituted a judicial committee headed by D.K. Jain, a retired Supreme Court judge, to "find out the ways and means to take appropriate steps against the erring officials."

A comprehensive picture of the ISRO espionage case right from its genesis would have emerged had the Supreme Court ordered for a judicial enquiry covering the entire gamut of the issue and its complexities.

But the case filed by Nambi Narayanan had no such prayer in it. His grievance was that the case had a catastrophic effect on his service career and life.

It is worth noting that all these years, Nambi Narayanan had objected to a judicial enquiry into the whole issue, whenever such a prayer came up before Kerala High Court in the form of a PIL.

Let us see the factuality behind Nambi Narayanan's case that Siby Mathews and other members of SIT inflicted a catastrophic effect on his service career and life.

Nambi Narayanan has no case that Siby Mathews or any member of the SIT had tortured him, physically or mentally, under whose custody he was for five days, and his interrogation by the SIT chief Siby Mathews "just lasted for one-and-a-half minutes".[75]

Moreover, the main accusation of CBI against Siby Mathews in its confidential letter to the Chief Secretary, Government of Kerala[76] is that Siby Mathews "left the entire investigation to IB, surrendering his duties."

UO note no 303/DIB/DESP/ 94[77] and UO note no 9/ESP/(U)94(3)-11-309[78] sent by the Director, IB, to the Cabinet Secretary and Home Minister, Government of India, make it clear that IB was directing Kerala police in the investigation of the espionage case; while Confidential Letter[79] sent by V.R. Rajeevan, Commissioner of Police, Trivandrum, to the DGP, Kerala, tells Kerala police was acting under dictation of IB.

In its confidential letter[80] addressed to the Secretary, Ministry of Home Affairs, Government of India, wherein CBI details the misdeeds of the IB officials, CBI states, "IB tortured/ ill-treated... Nambi Narayanan... and was given medical treatment on 3 December 1994, which is indicative of the torture".

The letter further reads:

> *...facts show that the aforesaid IB officials comprising the team enquiring into the ISRO case acted in an unprofessional manner and were privy to the arrest of six innocent persons, thereby*

---

75. *Deccan Herald*, September 17, 2018
76. Letter No. 2783/3/11(S) 94—SIU V/SIC, dated 3 June 1996
77. Dated 21 November 1994
78. Dated 28 November 1994
79. No. SB/1053/G1/94—TC (dated 24 October 1994)
80 No 2782/3/11(S) 94—SIU V/SIC (dated 3 June 1996),

causing them immense mental and physical agony ... At the IB HQ, the UO notes referred to herein were prepared based on these interrogation reports and without verification, leading to serious complications including casting doubts on the integrity of two top ISRO scientists who were responsible for developing the PSLV project and launching our country into space.

The note further states R.B. Sreekumar, Dy. Director, SIB, Trivandrum, and a member of the IB team that interrogated the accused, *"admitted that IB does not have the legal authority to examine the accused when they are in the custody of the police authority."*

Even then, Nambi Narayanan has no case against the IB officials!

He invoked the names of one or two IB officers only once, in 2000, when he filed a suit[81], before the Sub Court, Thiruvananthapuram, seeking damages to the tune of Rs. 1 crore. Though his suit was against the officials in both Kerala Police and IB and against the Kerala government and the Union government, Kerala government, in 2019, offered him Rs.1.3 crores for an out-of-court settlement[82].

Nambi Narayanan withdrew the suit, unconditionally, agreeing to no further claim against any of the defendants and that *"no personal liability can be fixed on the officials accused of falsely implicating him."*

It is intriguing that he won't make any move against the IB officers who tortured him; would get impleaded in any petition for a Judicial Enquiry in the matter and would argue against it (He did it twice before the Kerala High court), and wants legal action only against certain selected SIT members of the Kerala Police under whose custody he was only for five days; against whom he has no

---

81. O.S. No. 370/2003
82. GO (MS) No 203/2019 Home, dated 27/12/2019

case of inflicting torture on him, and who interrogated him only for *"one and a half minutes."*

Turning a blind eye towards IB is a calculated approach to ensure no enquiry should go beyond the scope of the SIT members of Kerala Police because an enquiry into the activities of IB, especially against the top brass, he fears, would end up in opening the can of worms; something he is worried about since the can has a worm that would narrate the story of a failed reverse espionage in which he had a lead role. He doesn't want it to happen. He wants the truth to rise only up to that level where he is safe in his comfort zone.

Similarly, Nambi Narayanan didn't file criminal or civil defamation case against any of the newspapers or magazines that painted him as a spy, womanizer, drunkard, and a lot more. He didn't ask the journalists who came for his interview—even after CBI had found the case "false and baseless"—that they should first apologize for the damage they had caused to his reputation. Instead, he became their darling with access allowed to anyone who approached him for an interview or for a video bite. The very same media that once branded him a spy took a complete U-turn by featuring him as a great scientist and a true patriot devastated by the espionage case.

The Orbit of Lies

Nambi Narayanan plays a totally different game with the media.

"I want people who fabricated this case against me to be punished. One chapter is over, but the next chapter is still there."[83].

"The alleged role of the CIA in fabricating the espionage case should be investigated...the role of the police, IB, politicians, the media, and the CIA should be probed."[84]

---

83. www.bbc.com/news/world-asia-india 27 Jan 2020

84. *The New Indian Express*, September 25, 2018

Nambi Narayanan would even present himself as the target of the espionage case: *"The conspirators had identified me as their target before starting the investigation."*[85]

But he wouldn't tell you why?

Let us see how he paints his picture in the public domain.

The SLP filed by Nambi Narayanan before the Supreme Court reads:

> *It is urged by the appellant that the prosecution launched against him by Kerala police was malicious on account of two reasons, the first being that the said prosecution had a catastrophic effect on his service career as a leading and renowned scientist at ISRO thereby smothering his career, life span, savings, honour, academic work as well as self-esteem and consequently resulting in total devastation of the peace of his entire family which is an ineffaceable individual loss, and the second, the irreparable and irremediable loss and setback caused to the technological advancement in Space Research in India.*

What Nambi Narayanan had stated before the Supreme Court in his SLP is a mixture of truths, lies, and contrived truths.

The statement that the spy case had affected his life and "consequently resulting in total devastation of the peace of (Nambi Narayanan's) entire family which is an ineffaceable individual loss" is a painful truth.

His claim that the case had a "catastrophic effect on his service career" is a blatant lie.

His statement that the case had caused "irreparable and irremediable loss and setback caused to the technological advancement in Space Research in India" is a contrived truth.

---

85. *The New Indian Express*, December 25, 2018

Let us examine the lie and contrived truth in his SLP.

The claim that the espionage case "inflicted a catastrophic effect on his service career" is factually incorrect.

Reason: Nambi Narayanan had applied for retirement under the Voluntary Retirement Scheme (VRS) 29 days before he was arrested on 30 November 1994.

The VRS application dated 1 November 1994, reads: *Due to personal reasons, I wish to seek voluntary retirement from ISRO. I shall be extremely grateful, if Chairman ISRO/ Secretary, DOS can condone and waive the retirement of three months notice and relieve me with effect from 11 November 1994.*

In the letter addressed ISRO chairman/ Secretary, department of Space, there is a handwritten portion that reads: *"Incidentally, you may kindly recall my discussion with you during August 94, my interest to seek voluntary retirement after the PSLV launch, and you had kindly agreed to my request to relieve me after the launch."*

And he had reasons for opting for VRS that had nothing, whatsoever, to do with the espionage case. In his own words, "In April 1994, K .Kasturirangan assumed office as the Chairman of ISRO. I was the Deputy Director of VSSC. Our Director was the senior-most person eligible for the post of Chairman, and I had expected a promotion as Director. I had informed the Chairman in advance that I will opt for VRS if I don't get the promotion."[86]

In other words, Nambi Narayanan had decided to quit ISRO in April 1994 if he doesn't get promoted as Director. His decision to quit ISRO was personal and professional.

To put it mildly, Nambi Narayanan told a lie to the Supreme Court that the espionage case had "a catastrophic effect on his service career as a leading and renowned scientist at ISRO" since he had put

86. Newsroom 24X7.com, 4 May 2021

in his papers for VRS 29 days before he was arrested and had made up his mind to quit ISRO seven months before he was arrested.

A clear case of perjury!

Moreover, the case didn't "smother" his career because he was promoted to Director, Advanced Technology and Planning, and was posted in ISRO Head Office in Bangalore, reporting directly to Chairman, ISRO.

Does he mean the case had spoiled his chances of becoming the Chairman, ISRO?

But then, how could he have dreamed of becoming the Chairman, ISRO, after opting for VRS on 1 November 1994?

The second part of his statement before the Supreme Court is that "the prosecution launched against him by Kerala police caused an irreparable and irremediable loss and setback caused to the technological advancement in Space Research in India."

See, he presents the whole case as a prosecution launched against him! Where have the five other accused gone? Even their identities have been effaced.

Even if you accept his stand, was it not the failed misadventure of ISRO to get the cryogenic technology transferred from Glavkosmos through reverse espionage (in which Prof. U.R. Rao, S. Nambi Narayanan, and D. Sasikumaran had lead roles) that brought the CIA to the scene with an absurd espionage story?

What was the role of ISRO and what, specifically, was Nambi Narayanan's role in the illegal and clandestine operation?

Doesn't it sound sensible that both ISRO and the technocrats (who were instrumental in attempting reverse espionage) owe an apology to the nation?

Instead, Nambi Narayanan intentionally airs lies to insulate the Glavkosmos- Url Aviation-ISRO trajectory from being probed. A report in Open Magazine (11 March 2016) reads: *Narayanan remembers that Air India had refused to carry the shipments from Moscow, arguing that the airline may be blacklisted by the US for doing so. It was why he had to hire Ural Airlines to carry "what was a legal cargo supplied by Russians under the contract".*

The reasoning for Air India's refusal, questions your intelligence.

Why should the US blacklist Air India for carrying the *"legal cargo supplied by Russians under the contract"*?

Why should the US blacklist Air India for carrying legal cargo from Russia when the US had no objection to the second agreement that didn't have the technology clause?

Was Url Aviation not worried about such blacklisting by the US?

Why did Url take the risk for ISRO, which Air India chose not to?

The fact is that Nambi Narayanan is confusing the people who still have questions about the whole episode.

However, he admits he was the man who engaged Url to carry the cargo which Air India had refused to carry, but insulates the whole operation by terming the cargo as "legal… and supplied by Russians under the contract."

Now, Nambi Narayanan and ISRO need to specify under which contract – the first or the second?

The first was scrapped in July 1993. The second, signed in January 1994, had no technology transfer clause.

Importantly, the first engine under the second agreement was to reach India only in 1996.

All the three Url Aviation flights reached India after ISRO signed the second agreement – that didn't have the technology transfer clause—with Glavkosmos.

Does Nambi Narayanan want us to believe the cargo was the cryogenic engines as part of legal delivery under the new agreement signed in January 1994?

If so, why did Air India object to take them?

Does it mean the first flight with the engine was transported to India on the very same month the second agreement was signed? (The first Url flight that had S. Nambi Narayanan on board reached Thiruvananthapuram airport on 23 January 1994)

If it was part of a "legal cargo supplied by Russians under the contract", as Nambi Narayanan claims, why didn't the fourth flight of Url Aviation come?

Now, who did the maximum damage to India?

The CIA, which planted the espionage story?

Top brass in IB who worked as moles of CIA?

Russia, which cancelled the 1991 contract under American pressure and accepted booty from America, in return?

Or the ISRO- technocrats—with the approval of ISRO management and Space Commission— whose illegal act of 'patriotism' nosedived?

People have been pushed into a world of conjectures, with a lot of questions remaining unanswered.

ISRO and the Government of India need to tell the people to what extent the misfired 'patriotic' adventure has cost ISRO in terms of money, especially when the business from the space market is expected to touch $558 billion by 2026 and up to $ 1.75 trillion by 2040.

It is high time the ISRO and the government of India come clean on the matter. If both parties confirm this operation was in the interest of the nation and hence need to be treated as brave acts of 'patriotism', a different picture would emerge.

But then, one needs to deconstruct the very concept of patriotism.

References

Confidential letter no. 46/CAD/CRH/94 dated November 30, 1994 signed by Siby Mathews IPS and addressed to the Director General of Police.

Confidential Letter No. SB/1053/01/94-TC dated October 24, 1994 signed by V.R. Rajeevan, IPS to the Director General of Police.

http://classic.austlii.edu.au/au/journals/FedLawRw/1985/5.pdf

https://www.mondaq.com/india/trials-appeals-compensation/905712/alibi--a-conundrum-between-prosecution-and-accused

Judgment of Kerala High Court in Crl. R.P. No. 437/96 delivered on November 27, 1996.

Judgment of Kerala High Court in Crl, R.P.: 437/96 delivered on November 27, 1996.

Judgment of Kerala High Court in O.P. No. 12747 (and others), 1996, delivered on November 27, 1996.

Judgment of the Kerala High Court in O.P. No. 16358 delivered on November 27, 1996.

Judgment of the Kerala High Court in W.A. No. 1676/94—C (in O.P. No. 17367 of 1994—P) Niyamavedi v. CBI delivered on January 13, 1995.

Judgment of the Kerala High Court in W.A. No. 1676/94—C (in O.P. No. 17367 of 1994—P) Niyamavedi v. CBI, delivered on January 13, 1995.

Judgment of the Kerala High Court in W.A. No. 1676/94—C (in O.P. No. 17367 of 1994—P) Niyamavedi v. CBI, delivered on January 13, 1995.

Letter No: 2782/3/11 (5) 94—SIU Ai/SIC—ill dated June 3, 1996 to the Secretary, Ministry of Home Affairs, Government of India.

Letter No: 2783/3/11 (S) 94-SIU V/S1C—III dated June 3, 1996 to the Chief Secretary, Government of Kerala.

Maharaj V. Attorney General of Trinidad and Tobago (1978) quoted in Ega Venkaiah V. Judges, David Pannick, Oxford University Press, 1987, p. 1.

Malayala Manorma, dated August 24, 1997.

Malyala Manorama, dated August 27, 1997.

Mrs. Susheela Misra v. Delhi Ad-ministration (1984) 1 SCC 202 at p. 203; 1984 Crimes 142. The Supreme Court of India has held that "the questioning, by exercise of power conferred by section 8 of the IOS Act, 1923 must be during the day time and in no case after sun-set and before sunrise."

Newsroom 24X7, https://newsroom24x7.com//police-officers-behind-fake-isro-spy-case-should-be-tried-for-treason-justicefornambinarayanan

NHRC (Law division) Letter No, 11 /27/96—LC, dated January 15, 1997.

Order of the Chief Judicial Magistrate, Ernakulam, in C.C. No. 1464/94 delivered on November 14, 1995.

Order of the Chief Judicial Magistrate, Trivandrum in Crl. M.P. No. 10029 in Crime No. 246/94, Vanchiyoor Police Station, delivered on December 13, 1996.

Order of the Court of Sessions in Cr1. M.C. No. 1538 delivered on September 6, 1997.

Order of the Court of Sessions in Crl. M.C. No. 1529/97 delivered on September 6, 1997.

Petition to the Chief Justice of India dated February 1, 1997.

Petition to the Kerala State Women's Commission dated July 23, 1997.

Petition to the National Human Rights Commission dated July 19, 1996.

Savvy, April '96 issue.

The Hindu, August 19, 1997.

The Hindu, dated August 26, 1997.

List of acronyms

ADE	–	Aeronautical Defence Establishment
CBI	–	Central Bureau of Investigation
CIA	–	Central Intelligence Agency
CJM	–	Chief Judicial Magistrate
CPI (M)	–	Communist Party of India (Marxist)
CrPC	–	Code of Criminal Procedure
DIB	–	Director IB
DRDO	–	Defence Research Development Organisation
FIR	–	First Information Report
GATT	–	General Agreement on Tariffs and Trade
HMT	–	Hindustan Machine Tools
IB	–	Intelligence Bureau
IOS Act	–	Indian Official Secrets Act
ISRO	–	Indian Space Research Organisation
KSWC	–	Kerala State Women's Commission
LDF	–	Left Democratic Front
LPSC	–	Liquid Propellant Systems Centre
MTAR	–	Managing Partner of Machine Tools Aid and Reconditioning
NHRC	–	National Human Rights Commission
SHAR	–	Sriharikota Range
SIT	–	Special Investigation Team
SLP	–	Special Leave Petition
UO note	–	unofficial note

Recommended Reading

BEYOND REASONABLE DOUBT

Ranjit Mishra

When Salman Curtis set foot on the steamer bound from London to Calcutta, he had no inkling of the adventures that awaited him as an Anglo-Indian police officer.

His postings take him from sleepy villages to bustling towns, from *panchayats* to court rooms, from investigating petty crimes to heart-wrenching murders and dacoity. This book describes some of the most horrifying crimes he becomes a witness to.

Unfolding the life and times of late 19th century India, *Beyond Reasonable Doubt* is a well-researched compendium of investigations undertaken under the British Raj, which laid the foundation for many crime-solving methods used till date.

Ranjit Mishra is an I.P.S. Officer of 2007 batch, Bihar cadre. He has over 14 years of experience in law enforcement, crime control, anti-Naxal operations and law & order maintenance. He has served as Superintendent of Police in over half a dozen districts in Bihar.

ISBN: 978-9390441723, Pages: 232, MRP: 350, Format: Paperback

DEATH SERVED COLD

Sourabh Mukherjee

A woman relishes the last cries of her husband on the phone as he is brutally murdered by her lover. A teenager poisons her family for the love of her tutor. A woman driven by greed ruthlessly bludgeons eight members of her family.

A beautician gangs up with her lover to rob a house, killing innocent women from three generations of a family. A practising lawyer strangles her lawyer husband with the cord of a mobile charger. A friendly and jovial teacher commits at least six murders over fourteen years in a sleepy town down south.

DEATH SERVED COLD is a painstakingly researched collection of true, blood-curdling accounts of gruesome murders committed by India's most dangerous women over the last three decades.

Sourabh Mukherjee has written two psychological thriller novels and three short story collections appreciated by readers, critics and the media.

ISBN 978-9390441518, Pages: 216, MRP: 250, Format: Paperback